ASHE Higher Education Report: Volume 43, Number 5
Kelly Ward, Lisa E. Wolf-Wendel, Series Editors

Learning Analytics in Higher Education

Jaime Lester,

Carrie Klein,

Huzefa Rangwala,

Aditya Johri

Learning Analytics in Higher Education
Jaime Lester, Carrie Klein, Huzefa Rangwala, Aditya Johri
ASHE Higher Education Report: Volume 43, Number 5
Series Editors: Kelly Ward, Lisa E. Wolf-Wendel

ASHE HIGHER EDUCATION REPORT, (Print ISSN: 1551-6970; Online ISSN: 1554-6306), is published quarterly by Wiley Subscriptio Services, Inc., a Wiley Company, 111 River St., Hoboken, NJ 07030-5774 USA.
Postmaster: Send all address changes to *ASHE HIGHER EDUCATION REPORT*, John Wiley & Sons Inc., C/O The Sheridan Press, PO Box 46⁵ Hanover, PA 17331 USA.

Information for subscribers
ASHE HIGHER EDUCATION REPORT is published in 6 issues per year. Institutional subscription prices for 2017 are:
Print & Online: US$477 (US), US$557 (Canada & Mexico), US$626 (Rest of World), €406 (Europe), £323 (UK). Prices are exclusive of tax. Asia Pacific GST, Canadian GST/HST and European VAT will be applied at the appropriate rates. For more information on current tax rates, please g to www.wileyonlinelibrary.com/tax-vat. The price includes online access to the current and all online back-files to January 1st 2013, where available For other pricing options, including access information and terms and conditions, please visit www.wileyonlinelibrary.com/access.

Delivery Terms and Legal Title
Where the subscription price includes print issues and delivery is to the recipient's address, delivery terms are **Delivered at Place (DAP)**; the recipient is responsible for paying any import duty or taxes. Title to all issues transfers FOB our shipping point, freight prepaid. We will endeavor to fulfil claims for missing or damaged copies within six months of publication, within our reasonable discretion and subject to availability.

Back issues: Single issues from current and recent volumes are available at the current single issue price from cs-journals@wiley.com.

Disclaimer
The Publisher and Editors cannot be held responsible for errors or any consequences arising from the use of information contained in this journal; the views and opinions expressed do not necessarily reflect those of the Publisher and Editors, neither does the publication of advertisements constitute any endorsement by the Publisher and Editors of the products advertised.

Publisher: ASHE HIGHER EDUCATION REPORT is published by Wiley Periodicals, Inc., 350 Main St., Malden, MA 02148-5020.

Journal Customer Services: For ordering information, claims and any enquiry concerning your journal subscription please go to www.wileycustomerhelp.com/ask or contact your nearest office.
Americas: Email: cs-journals@wiley.com; Tel: +1 781 388 8598 or +1 800 835 6770 (toll free in the USA & Canada).
Europe, Middle East and Africa: Email: cs-journals@wiley.com; Tel: +44 (0) 1865 778315.
Asia Pacific: Email: cs-journals@wiley.com; Tel: +65 6511 8000.
Japan: For Japanese speaking support, Email: cs-japan@wiley.com.
Visit our Online Customer Help available in 7 languages at www.wileycustomerhelp.com/ask

Production Editor: Abha Mehta (email: abmehta@wiley.com).

Wiley's Corporate Citizenship initiative seeks to address the environmental, social, economic, and ethical challenges faced in our business and which are important to our diverse stakeholder groups. Since launching the initiative, we have focused on sharing our content with those in need, enhancing community philanthropy, reducing our carbon impact, creating global guidelines and best practices for paper use, establishing a vendor code of ethics, and engaging our colleagues and other stakeholders in our efforts. Follow our progress at www.wiley.com/go/citizenship

View this journal online at wileyonlinelibrary.com/journal/aehe

Wiley is a founding member of the UN-backed HINARI, AGORA, and OARE initiatives. They are now collectively known as Research4Life, making online scientific content available free or at nominal cost to researchers in developing countries. Please visit Wiley's Content Access - Corporate Citizenship site: http://www.wiley.com/WileyCDA/Section/id-390082.html

Printed in the USA by The Sheridan Group.

Address for Editorial Correspondence: Coeditors-in -chief, Kelly Ward, Lisa E. Wolf-Wendel, ASHE HIGHER EDUCATION REPORT, Email: lwolf@ku.edu and kaward@wsu.edu

Abstracting and Indexing Services
The Journal is indexed by Academic Search Alumni Edition (EBSCO Publishing); Education Index/Abstracts (EBSCO Publishing); ERIC: Educational Resources Information Center (CSC); Higher Education Abstracts (Claremont Graduate University); IBR & IBZ: International Bibliographies of Periodical Literature (KG Saur).

Cover design: Wiley
Cover Images: ©

For submission instructions, subscription and all other information visit:
wileyonlinelibrary.com/journal/aehe

Advisory Board

The ASHE Higher Education Report Series is sponsored by the Association for the Study of Higher Education (ASHE), which provides an editorial advisory board of ASHE members.

Contents

Executive Summary   9

Acknowledgements   15

Foreword   16

**Introduction to Learning Analytics and Educational Technology
Tools in Higher Education**   18
    Introduction   20
    Purpose of the Monograph   22
    Current Trends in Higher Education   23
    Status of Learning Analytics Research in Higher Education   29
    Framework for Examining Learning Analytics in Higher
      Education   32
      Organizational Theory   33
      Technology Alignment and Adoption   34
      Faculty and Advisor Beliefs and Behaviors   34
      Student Use and Action   35
      Ethics and Privacy   36
    Outline of the Monograph   37

**How Organizational Context and Capacity and Technological
Alignment Affect Learning Analytics Adoption**   38
    Introduction   39
    An Organizational Model for Individual Decision Making   42
      Individual Factors   43
      Institutional Levels   44
      Institutional Levers   45

Organizational Context   46
   Organizational Change   47
   Institutional Logics   48
   Organizational Readiness and Capacity   50
Technology Adoption and Alignment   52
   Technology Adoption Models   52
      Traditional Adoption Models   52
      Education-Focused Adoption Models 53
   Technology Alignment   55
Conclusion and Future Work   57

**Faculty, Advisor, and Student Decision Making Related to Use
of Learning Analytics Data and Tools**   **58**
   Introduction   60
Faculty and Advisor Decision Making   61
   Professional Identity   62
   Professional Beliefs   63
   Professional Behaviors   64
   Impact of Identity, Beliefs, and Behavior and Future Work   66
Student Decision Making   67
   Learning Analytics Dashboards   67
   Impact of Learning Analytics Dashboards on Student Actions   69
      Sensemaking and Trust   71
Conclusion and Future Work   73

Ethical and Privacy Concepts and Considerations   **74**
   Introduction   76
Ethics and Privacy: Definitions, Conceptions, and Influences   78
   Evolving Definitions and Concepts   79
   Ethics and Privacy Within the Higher Education Context   82
Institutional, Individual, and Data Considerations   83
   Institutional Contexts   83
   Individual Contexts   85
      Consent and Agency   86

Trust and Bias   87
Data Considerations   88
  Algorithmic Bias   88
  Transparency and Trust   89
  Security, Access, and Ownership   90
Laws, Policies, and Codes of Practice   91
  Laws and Regulations   91
  Policies and Recommendations   94
  Challenges in Practice   95
  Emerging Codes of Practice   96
Conclusion and Future Work   98

**Recommendations for Moving Forward: Considerations of
Organizational Complexity, Data Fidelity, and Future
Research**   **100**
Learning Analytics in Higher Education: Model Considerations
  and Recommendations   101
  Organizational Logic, Leadership, and Value   101
  Faculty and Advisor Input, Trust, and Engagement   104
  College Student Interpretation of and Context for Data   107
  Ethics and Privacy: Transparency and Ownership   110
Data Concerns and Recommendations   113
  Data Access, Provenance, and Fidelity   113
  Use-Case/Scenario-Based Design of Systems   114
  Work Practice Integration of Systems   114
  Personalized Information to Stakeholders   115
  Use-Inspired Research in Pasteur's Quadrant: Integrated
    Education, Research, and Advising   115
  Privacy, Accountability, Transparency, Security, and Trust 116
Suggestions for Future Research   116
  Quasiexperimental Design of Intervention Impacts   117
  Modeling Student Engagement   117

Modeling and Visualizing Student Learning Preferences
      and Prior Learning Outcomes   118
   Developing Ethical Codes of Practice and Use   119
   Conclusion   121

Resources   **122**

References   **125**

Name Index   **137**

Subject Index   **143**

About the Authors   **147**

Executive Summary

IN 2003, 5 BILLION gigabytes of data had been collected since the beginning of recorded history; today, 5 billion gigabytes of data can be collected in 10 seconds (Zwitter, 2014, p. 2). The Internet is full of facts on how much data are created daily and projections on how much will be collected in the future. Whether the numbers are entirely correct, industrialized countries are now in the era of big data, which are often defined by three characteristics: volume, variety, and velocity (Laney, 2001). Combined, these three characteristics indicate that big data have a high degree of volume (large in size), are real time or timely, and contain a variety of measures (DeMauro, Greco, & Grimaldi, 2016; Ylijoki & Porras, 2016). More succinctly stated, "Big data is a generic term that assumes that the information or database system(s) used as the main storage facility is capable of storing large quantities of data longitudinally and down to very specific transactions" (Picciano, 2012, p. 12). In the context of higher education, big data are ubiquitous in the form of student transcripts that contain course-level information, student college application data (in other words, SAT and ACT test scores, high school grade point averages and location), data on wireless Internet access, interactions with learning management systems (LMS), and, more recently, when students swipe their student identification cards for meals or access to buildings.

Learning analytics has evolved in education alongside the explosion of the big data revolution as a specific form of educational data mining. Although there is not a uniformly accepted definition of learning analytics, multiple sources tend to have the similar elements of statistical analysis, prediction, and requirements of large (commonly referred to as *big*) data. For the purposes of this monograph, we adopt the definition of the "measurement, collection, analysis and reporting of data about learners and their contexts, for purposes of understanding and optimizing learning and the environments in which it occurs" (Siemens & Gašević, 2012, p. 1). Essentially, learning analytics is the form of educational data mining that performs predictive analysis on big data with the intention of creating platforms for intervention. Learning analytics can also involve exploratory analysis that leads to the generation of new hypotheses associated with learning behaviors and habits.

Learning analytics, by their volume, timeliness, and composition, "expands the capacity and ability of organizations to make sense of complex environments" and promises to improve pedagogy, course design, student retention, and decision making by providing personalized feedback for users (Ali, Hatala, Gašević, & Jovanović, 2012; Macfadyen & Dawson, 2012; Norris & Baer, 2013, p. 13). This promise is alluring to higher education institutions, which are facing increasing pressure to provide evidence of student learning in an environment in which teaching pedagogical best practices are moving to an increasingly individualized and student-focused learning model and in which innovative technologies are allowing for greater mining of student data (Austin & Sorcinelli, 2013). Within this context, learning and advising management systems, based on educational big data, or learning analytics, are being developed to better measure, analyze, report, and predict data related to student learning, retention, and completion. These learning analytics-informed systems have the potential to generate new insight into courses and student learning by creating responsive feedback mechanisms that can shape data-informed decision making as it relates to teaching, learning, and advising.

Given the potential and increasing presence of learning analytics in higher education, it is important to understand what it is, what associated barriers and opportunities exist, and how it can be used to improve organizational and individual practices, including strategic planning, course development, teaching pedagogy, and student advising. The purpose of this monograph is to give readers a practical and theoretical foundation in learning analytics in higher education, including an understanding of the challenges and incentives that are present in the institution, in the individual, and in the technologies themselves.

Among questions that are explored and answered are:

1. What are the current trends in higher education that are driving a need for learning analytics tools?
2. What role do institutional context, technological capacity, and individual beliefs play in promoting or constraining adoption and integration of learning analytics technologies in higher education?
3. What are the ethical considerations related to use of learning analytics or other predictive data and associated interventions?
4. What are the practical implications and future research recommendations associated with learning analytics?

Organized into five chapters, this monograph is intended to serve as an introduction to learning analytics for those practitioners and researchers who are interested in learning more about the development, implementation, and promise of harnessing educational big data with predictive methods. We also complicate learning analytics in higher education by drawing attention to the complex ethical and privacy issues surrounding the collection and dissemination of such data. Although the issues are far from simple, there are considerations and questions that can guide development and practical use of learning analytics tools.

Learning analytics as a field is new and emerging. The major association Learning Analytics & Knowledge has existed for less than 10 years; theoretical frameworks and research literature are just now beginning to emerge in large quantities. As with all new fields, learning analytics has drawn from a number of multidisciplinary trends and literatures to examine different facets of use, design, and implementation but has yet to bring together the complexity of external and internal organizational factors; faculty, advisor, and student motivation to use learning analytics; and ethics and privacy concerns. This monograph draws from several areas of research—organizational theory, technology adoption, faculty beliefs and behaviors, and ethics and privacy—in a comprehensive model of learning analytics in higher education. Our model conceptualizes adoption of learning analytics in higher education as being done within the context of organizational factors (for example, infrastructure, change readiness, and so on) with ethics and privacy underlying all other areas; meaning, ethics, and privacy should be the guidepost for all decision making regarding learning analytics. The purpose of this model is to identify the complex issues surrounding adoption of learning analytics in higher education that is often noted as a challenge in the literature that takes into account the organizational, technological, individual, and ethics literature.

The first chapter provides an overview of the monograph and of the issues related to use of learning analytics in higher education, including information on what learning analytics is, the environmental context that has contributed to the emergence and evolution of the use of learning analytics in higher education, how analytics are currently being used in higher education, and some of the unique challenges and opportunities learning analytics systems face in higher education settings. In this chapter, we present the framework for learning analytics in higher education with a brief overview of each tenet of the model. Subsequent chapters provide extensive review of the literature and discussion of the model. The chapter concludes with an introduction to the structure and purpose of the remaining chapters.

The second chapter focuses on organizational aspects of the learning analytics in higher education model with a brief review of the literature on organizational change, institutional logics, and capacity and readiness related to learning analytics tools in higher education. We argue that organizational factors that create barriers and opportunities for learning analytics implementation and adoption in higher education are rooted in issues of institutional structures, commitment, resources, readiness, and capacity and a lack of incentives and rewards (Arnold, Lonn, & Pistilli, 2014; Austin, 2011; Bichsel, 2012; Kezar & Lester, 2009; Macfadyen & Dawson, 2012; Norris & Baer, 2013). Implementation of learning analytics also requires attention to a host of technological factors including provision of data, technical data analytics expertise, cross-organization collaboration, leadership, and attention to organizational climate (Arnold et al., 2014; Bichsel, 2012; Ferguson, 2012; Klein,

Lester, Rangwala, & Johri, in press; Norris & Baer, 2013). The chapter concludes with an overview of technological aspects of learning analytics tools and individual decision making, including a review of innovation adoption and tool alignment.

In the third chapter, we focus on the aspects of individual decision making that exist within that context for faculty, advisors, and students who are increasingly interacting with learning analytics, whether or not they are aware of it. Data from learning management systems (LMS) (for example, Blackboard and Moodle) are being mined and incorporated into learning analytics algorithms that provide data visualizations and performance feedback related to teaching, advising, and course performance. LMS and learning analytics tools are examples of changing pedagogical innovations that have been deployed and leveraged as a way to improve institutional and individual decision making (Bichsel, 2012; Dahlstrom, Brooks, & Bichsel, 2014; Macfadyen & Dawson, 2012). However, these tools are useful to higher education only if individuals decide to adopt them. Engaging the theoretical models and research on faculty pedagogy change (Austin, 2011) and the work on learning analytics and student behaviors (Arnold & Pistilli, 2012), we argue that for faculty, advisors, and students the decision to engage in these tools is rooted in professional identity, beliefs, and behaviors and through learning analytics visualizations.

Emerging as a major consideration of learning analytics use in higher education are issues of ethics and privacy. The fourth chapter explores the challenges associated in creating analytics-based technologies as they relate to establishing an ethics of care and consent, respecting and maintaining privacy, and safeguarding against algorithmic bias and data insecurity, including an overview of ethical and privacy guidelines, laws, and policies; the choices related to including specific data points in learning analytics algorithms (especially demographic-based data); and the use of those data to predict student outcomes. Further, we review the privacy concerns related to collection, use, and ownership of student faculty and staff data and issues related to individual agency in an age of educational data mining.

In the final chapter of the monograph, we engage the framework proposed in the first chapter to look at how some of the issues associated with learning analytics in higher education can be mitigated and to consider the directions in which learning analytics needs to move in order for it to be transformational. The solutions, we believe, lie in thinking through the complexities of individual decision making, pedagogical change, organizational policies and practices, and data access, ethics, and privacy. Before any of these issues are a consideration, data must be available and of a high quality to build the tools. Simply, learning analytics tools cannot exist without data. And, like other issues, data come with their own set of complexities. We explore issues and provide specific recommendations on data and data use in learning analytics, such as data use and availability; importance of design thinking; and personalization in data visualization. The chapter concludes with suggestions for future research.

Acknowledgments

WE WOULD LIKE to thank Lisa Wolf-Wendel and Kelly Ward for the opportunity to contribute to the ASHE Higher Education Report series through the work of this monograph. Our research that is referenced in this monograph is supported in part by a grant from the National Science Foundation under grant IIS-1447489.

Foreword

B IG DATA ARE big news. One need not look far to see news reports
on how institutions around the globe are mining data to help improve
institutional functions. Higher education too is jumping on the "big data"
bandwagon, actively working on how to make use of faculty and student data
to improve outcomes. The topic is important and timely. As such, it is with
great pleasure that I present this monograph on *Learning Analytics in Higher
Education* by Jaime Lester, Carrie Klein, Huzefa Rangwala, and Aditya Johri
as part of the ASHE Higher Education Report series.

Learning analytics (LA)—the use of educational "big data" to analyze and
predict student learning and success—holds great promise for higher education. This promise, however, has yet to be fully realized because we haven't
fully tapped into its potential and figured out how to harness it to truly
help students. The present monograph explores these and related issues—
explaining what LA are, how they work, the associated barriers and opportunities that LA provides, and how it can be harnessed to improve student
learning. The monograph offers practical and theoretical understanding of
learning analytics, building on the small but growing empirical literature that
is available on the subject.

This monograph is sure to be of interest to those who study topics related to student outcomes, assessment, institutional research, and institutional
effectiveness. This monograph will be of interest to institutional researchers,
student affairs administrators, provosts, deans, and others with responsibilities related to the assessment of student outcomes. Researchers in the field,
both senior level and graduate students, are also bound to learn a lot from

this monograph that will be of use. Most important, the monograph is geared toward faculty members and advisors who find themselves on the frontlines of implementing, adopting, and integrating LA into their work with students.

As the monograph explains, "Learning analytics provide personalized, real-time, actionable feedback through mining and analysis of large data sets, which can illuminate trends and predict future outcomes that may not be visible via smaller data sets." The authors caution, however, that the adoption of learning analytics tools is expensive and fraught with challenges—including how to make the data meaningful to those who need to use it most (that is, decision makers, faculty members, advisors, and students). The purpose of this monograph is to delve into the research, literature, and issues associated with learning analytics implementation, adoption, and use by individuals within higher education institutions. Through the use of vignettes and a summary of relevant research and theory, the authors clearly outline what is happening with regard to LA in institutions of higher education, its future potential in the field, along with an important consideration of ethical and privacy concepts and concerns. This is a "must read" for everyone in the field. Big data are here to stay—so we had best figure out how to use them in a thoughtful manner or they will do more harm than good. This monograph helps readers work their way through the complexities of the issues and figure out practical next and future steps.

Introduction to Learning Analytics and Educational Technology Tools in Higher Education

Julie is a second-semester student majoring in computer science. She is having a successful first year, having earned high grades in all of her introductory courses and is beginning to plan for the fall semester. The university has been advertising a new learning analytics tool that has current updates on student course grades, assignments due in class, and future course planning. As a computer science major, Julie has some knowledge of the predictive analytics behind the tool and logs on to see what it is all about. To Julie's surprise, the tool has all of her information, including grades on all her assignments, extracurricular activities she attended, and even potential grades she will receive in future major and general education courses. She takes this information and begins planning her fall semester when she gets an email from her psychology course teaching assistant asking to speak with her during class this week. The teaching assistant notes that Julie had done poorly on her first quiz and wants to follow up on the material and her study habits. Julie is surprised that she did not do well but is willing to talk to the teaching assistant.

Professor Smith enters her office in University Hall and sits down at her computer to begin planning for the second meeting of her introductory psychology course, a course with over 200 students in a lecture hall. She opens her Internet browser and logs on to the university learning analytics tool. Last week, her students completed a quiz of the readings, the grades from which are being compared to each student's prior grade point average (GPA) and skill competency level. Professor Smith can look at each individual student's performance but prefers to look at the aggregate scores to determine whether she needs to review certain concepts or move on to the material planned for the week. Sure enough, only about half the students seem to understand motivation and those students all have prior coursework in psychology or a related field. Professor Smith makes a note to cover the material again and communicates with her teaching assistants about reinforcing the material in the discussion sections. Those students who did not do well on the first quiz are put on a watch list for the teaching assistants to follow up with to ensure they are learning the content and developing appropriate study skills.

A student knocks on the door. "Hi, we have an appointment at 2:30, right?" Angela, an advisor, gestures for the student to sit on the open chair in her small office in University Hall and says, "Of course, Julie, please do come in. We need to discuss what courses you want to take next semester." After a conversation about Julie's semester including her current skills, anticipated grades, and career plans, Angela logs on her computer, goes to the university learning analytics tool, and enters Julie's student identification number. Angela can see that Julie is taking three biology courses as well as one psychology course to meet her general education requirements. Angela notes that Julie has struggled a bit with her psychology course but did take the advice of the teaching instructor and sought additional help. In the last few weeks of the semester, Angela can see that Julie is on track to receive the predicted grades based on her assignment grades and is achieving competency in multiple skills areas. Angela turns the computer screen to Julie showing her how these courses are providing the necessary skills (also student learning outcomes) for her career path and what courses she may want to take next. Julie makes notes of the courses that will continue to develop her skills and keep her GPA high.

Introduction

In 2003, 5 billion gigabytes of data had been collected since the beginning of recorded history; today, 5 billion gigabytes of data can be collected in 10 seconds (Zwitter, 2014, p. 2). The Internet is full of predictions of how much data are created daily and how much will be collected in 5 or 10 years. Whether the numbers are entirely correct, industrialized countries are now in the era of big data, which are often defined by three characteristics: volume, variety, and velocity (Laney, 2001). Combined, these three characteristics indicate that big data have a high degree of volume (large in size), are real time or timely, and contain a variety of measures (DeMauro, Greco, & Grimaldi, 2016; Ylijoki & Porras, 2016). More succinctly stated, "Big data is a generic term that assumes that the information or database system(s) used as the main storage facility is capable of storing large quantities of data longitudinally and down to very specific transactions" (Picciano, 2012, p. 12). In the context of higher education, big data are ubiquitous in the form of student transcripts that contain course-level information, student college application data (in other words, SAT and ACT test scores, high school grade point averages and location), data on wireless Internet access, interactions with learning management systems (LMS), and, more recently, when students swipe their student identification cards for meals or access to buildings.

Learning analytics has evolved in education alongside the explosion of the big data revolution as a specific form of educational data mining. Although there is not a uniformly accepted definition of learning analytics, multiple sources tend to have the similar elements of statistical analysis, prediction, and requirements of large (commonly referred to as "big") data. For the purposes of this text, we adopt the definition of the "measurement, collection, analysis and reporting of data about learners and their contexts, for purposes of understanding and optimizing learning and the environments in which it occurs" (Siemens & Gašević, 2012, p.1). Essentially, learning analytics is the form of educational data mining that performs predictive analysis on big data with the intention of creating platforms for intervention, such as the tool Professor Smith used to identify students who were performing poorly and then to create interventions to assist students in successfully completing the course.

A report by EDUCAUSE (Arroway, Morgan, O'Keefe, & Yanosky, 2016) further complicates the definition of learning analytics by first referring to analytics as "the use of data, statistical analysis, and explanatory predictive models to gain insight and act on complex issues" (p. 7). Learning analytics is then the analytics applied to student success whereas institutional analytics applies to services and business operations in higher education institutions. The distinctions here are not trivial or academic; rather, learning analytics is a specific application of a more generic trend of statistical predictive analysis using big data to understand and to infer certain key characteristics about student learning, similar to the tool used by Angela to identify predicted grades in Julie's classes and advise her on her mastery of course learning outcomes. Other uses are related to connecting student learning to local career opportunities. Enrollment managers may adopt learning analytics tools, for example, that combine local or institutional service area economic data with demographic data from public schools to predict university application and yield (number of students who are admitted and enroll) numbers. Eduventures (2013) conducted a study of predictive analytics in higher education and noted in one such case study

> *The same administrator used predictive analytics at the dawn of the most recent economic recession. By studying not only internal institutional data but also data from New York City public schools and the Consumer Price Index, he was able to model the expected impact of the recession on the incoming fall class. With this advance information, he increased the size of the spring class to offset projected fall declines and saved $780,000 (p. 8).*

Another example of learning analytics is taking data from student use of LMS and predicting those variables that lead to increased student retention. Dawson, Macfadyen, and Lockyer (2009) found that students who engage in more discussion postings, send more email messages, and take more assessments had higher total grades in the course. These findings and others reviewed throughout this text identify how learning analytics can potentially inform student success and learning.

The rise of educational big data harnessed through learning analytics also coincides with student populations who are increasingly comfortable with technology-enhanced learning environments and demand more immediate real-time feedback. In the opening vignette, Julie was amenable to engaging in a tool that collected data on her course engagement as well as her activities on campus, which is common for students in her generation who grew up around technology that harnesses big data and algorithms. EDUCAUSE Center for Analysis and Research (Arroway et al., 2016) found in a national survey of undergraduate students and technology needs that student ownership and use of digital devices continue to grow each year with approximately only 1% of students not owning a device. In higher education learning environments, students also noted a preference for courses with some blended—face-to-face and online—elements and regularly engage with instructors who have knowledge of and success in connecting course material to online collaborative tools (Arroway et al., 2016). Importantly, EDUCAUSE also found that female and first-generation students experience increased engagement and enrichment as a result of technology use. These data points are important as higher education institutions welcome new generations of students who are expected to continue to engage in technologies from an early age, have increased comfort with online learning elements, and are more diverse in terms of race/ethnicity, gender, socioeconomic status, and academic preparation.

Purpose of the Monograph

This monograph is intended for anyone who works in higher education and uses learning management systems, especially those based on learning analytics algorithms. Information in the monograph will be relevant for faculty, advisors, and administrators who are interested in the potential and challenges related to implementation, adoption, and integration of these systems on their campuses and within their classrooms and advising sessions. Among questions that will be explored and answered are (a) What are the current trends in higher education that are driving a need for learning analytics tools?; (b) What roles do institutional context, technological capacity, and individual beliefs play in promoting or constraining adoption and integration of learning analytics technologies in higher education?; (c) What are the ethical considerations related to use of learning analytics or other predictive data and associated interventions?; and (d) What are the practical implications and future research recommendations associated with learning analytics? To situate these questions, we propose a multidisciplinary framework that brings together the literature on organizational studies, technology adoption, and faculty pedagogy change to conceptualize a framework to implement and research learning analytics in higher education.

We intend for this monograph to serve as an introduction to learning analytics for those practitioners and researchers who are interested in learning more about the development, implementation, and promise of harnessing educational big data with predictive methods. We also complicate learning analytics in higher education by drawing attention to the complex ethical and privacy issues surrounding the collection and dissemination of such data. Although the issues are far from simple, there are considerations and questions that can guide development and practical use of learning analytics tools. In the following, we identify the current trends in higher education that are driving the development and adoption of learning analytics, briefly summarize the current research, and propose a multidisciplinary framework for understanding learning analytics in higher education. As learning analytics is an emerging field, much of the research has developed across disparate disciplines with little integration.

Current Trends in Higher Education

Changes in student composition is just one of the challenges and considerations for higher education institutions. The ability to mine and analyze large amounts of institutional data is not just alluring but also useful for higher education institutions facing increasing environmental pressures to provide *proof* of learning, institutional accountability, and increased retention and completion rates. Higher education institutions across the country struggle with student retention and graduation. Although not always publicly revealed for each institution, national statistics indicate that 60% of students who begin their pursuit of a bachelor's degree graduate within 6 years (National Center for Education Statistics [NCES], 2016b). There is some variation by institutional type with 65% graduation rates at private nonprofit institutions, 58% at public nonprofit, and 27% at for-profit institutions (NCES, 2016a). The graduation numbers provide a long-term view of student success whereas retention rates, that is, the percentage of students who return from spring to fall, identify a more incremental measurement of student success. In 2014, the NCES (2016b) identified an 81% overall retention rate for all first-time, full-time degree seeking students. The retention numbers also varied by selectivity of institution with a 62% rate at the least selection, those institutions with open admissions, and 96% for the most selective, institutions that admitted less than 25% of applicants.

Importantly, the retention and graduation rates already reflect a historically successful group of students—those who attend higher education full time and have fewer outside college pressures, such as raising a family or working. A more accurate indicator of how students across the higher education enterprise are faring are the rates in community colleges who educate about half of all college students and have a majority student population who are part-time students, working full or part time, and have significant outside college personal responsibilities (Cohen, Brawer, & Kisker, 2013). The National Student Clearinghouse (2016) reported that retention rates for students who started at community colleges was 60% with a 69% rate for full-time and 55% for part-time students. Arguably, any institution would desire the graduation and retention rates to be closer to 100%.

Reasons for student success in retention and graduation are well researched in the higher education literature. A quick citation search for the foundational works of Tinto (1987), Astin (1993), and Kuh (2003) identifies more than 25,000 citations. Briefly, student–faculty interaction, engagement in academic and social activities, institutional climate, and prior academic experience and demographic variables affect student retention and graduation. Statistical models and qualitative studies have expanded and deepened knowledge of these factors, and others, using social science research methods. Learning analytics has already begun to provide data to support student success on two major fronts: (a) using predictive analytics to identify students who are likely to encounter challenges with retention and graduation (Picciano, 2012) and (b) real-time measures that signal when a student is exhibiting characteristics related to dropping out of a course or college all together (Arnold & Pistilli, 2012; Picciano, 2012). For example, the Purdue Course Signals Project began with the premise that students are not fully aware of how they are progressing in their courses and that midterm grades common on many college campuses are too late to intervene to help a student successfully complete a course (Arnold & Pistilli, 2012). Using predictive analytics based on "performance, effort, prior academic history and student characteristics" (Sclater, Peasgood, & Mullan, 2016, p. 1) Course Signals visualized student progress as traffic lights. The lights signaled to students how they were progressing—green gave students positive feedback with yellow and red providing negative feedback on student performance. In all cases, faculty could tailor their communications to assist students with either continuing their habits and behaviors in class or intervene to help students progress from yellow or red to a green light.

The higher education discourse is continuing to be influenced by vocationalism—educational philosophy arguing that curriculum should be focused on occupational opportunities—with an increased focus on student curricular pathways. Initially emphasized by former President Obama's American Graduation Initiative that called for 5 million additional graduates by 2020 to keep the United States on track as the world leader in education, many organizations took up this charge. This created a ground swell of activities around student curricular pathways with an emphasis on ways to identify the most efficient course-taking pathways. A recent book by Bailey, Jagger, and Jenkins (2015) represents the trend of student curricular pathways by arguing that community colleges need to adopt a curricular-guided pathways model to reduce the cafeteria style of course taking, wherein students can pick and choose classes. Bailey and colleagues explain that student course taking is often unclear with too many curricular options in the form of electives and course alternatives thus being more cafeteria in approach. The guided pathways would give students "who have chosen a major or program are provided with a program map that defines a default sequence of courses, each with clear learning outcomes that build across the curriculum into a coherent set of skills, which in turn aligned with requirements for successful transfer or career advancement" (p. 22). Similar initiatives, such as the Degree Qualification Profile (Adelman, Ewell, Gaston, & Geary Schneider, 2014) and Completion by Design (Nodine, Venezia, & Bracco, 2011), follow a similar argument that reducing curricular complexity and connecting courses and academic program to vocational skills and career advancement will help to achieve the goals of the American Graduation Initiative and similar, state-level goals. Although student transcript analysis and pathway research are not strictly new (Bahr, 2013; Hagedorn &DuBray, 2010), new methods, particularly those in engineering education and learning analytics, are revealing more on how to predict and advise student curricular pathways (Almatrafi, Rangwala, Johri, & Lester, 2016).

Another important trend in higher education that is related to learning analytics is the increased use of learning management systems and subsequent data analysis to identify the variables and behaviors that promote student success. LMS, discussed in more detail later in this chapter, are familiar to many who work in higher education but are essentially systems that provide an online platform with infrastructure and tools to manage and organize course material (Elbadrawy, Polyzou, Ren, Sweeney, Karypis, & Rangwala, 2016). Examples of LMS include Blackboard, Moodle, and Desire 2 Learn. National student survey data do suggest that LMS is regularly used by college students who note it is important to their success, particularly as a main communication device with faculty (Lang & Pirani, 2014).

Educational data mining research on LMS data has uncovered several important predictors on student success, namely the impact of engagement measures (for example, logins, number of forum posts, time online) on student course completion and final grade (Elbadrawy et al., 2016; Sweeney, Lester, & Rangwala, 2015). Campbell, Finnegan, and Collins (2006) in an examination of student academic success and LMS data found that student logins in the LMS were more predictive of student completion than SAT scores, an indicator of prior academic preparation. The authors also found that logging in the LMS, as a proxy for engagement in course material, leads to higher course grades even for those students who entered with low to moderate SAT scores. Macfadyen and Dawson (2010) conducted a similar study to Campbell and colleagues, finding that student activity in forum posting, email messages, logins, time spent online, and assessments (tests or quizzes) completed predicted students' final grades. Using a predictive model, Macfadyen and Dawson (2010) were also able to accurately predict student success in the course. A more recent study confirms the impact of engagement measures. Pursel, Zhang, Jablokow, Choi, and Velegol (2016) also identified in a study of massive open online course (MOOC) forum posts and comments to peers as predictors of student completion adding the additional element of communication with peers and not just the instructor. They also found that students who noted that they intended to highly engage in the course via a precourse survey did so and received a high grade, thus adding credibility to the notion that self-directed learning plays a role in online student success. In related context, Ren, Rangwala, and Johri (2016) developed a regression model to predict the grades for assessments for students enrolled in a MOOC, based on past performance.

Another prevalent trend in higher education that increasingly relies on data is assessment. Beginning on a larger scale with the 2001 federal legislation known as No Child Left Behind, an increased emphasis on measuring and reporting with the intent of federal and state accountability policies emerged. Although No Child Left Behind had an immediate and often viewed as negative (Jacob, 2005) impact on primary and secondary schools, higher education was also susceptible as national groups, accreditation associations, and individual campuses began to promote new mechanisms to document college student learning. For example, the Association of American Colleges and Universities (AAC&U) developed the Liberal Education and America's Promise (LEAP) project to identify student learning outcomes and rubrics for measurement. Community colleges ushered in the Voluntary Framework for Accountability as another example. Yet, one major challenge remains: how does an institution, college, or department systematically collect and analyze data on student learning given current fiscal and human resource constraints? Macfadyen, Dawson, Pardo, and Gašević (2014) suggest, "While current assessment policy may be driven by conflicting intentions—accountability and quality assurance requirements versus promotion of student learning—learning analytics can meet both. More simply put, learning analytics addresses the need for quality assurance and learning improvement" (p. 19). The authors acknowledge and provide frameworks for addressing the complexity of getting to a system that could meet accountability requirements but still acknowledge that learning analytics has much unrealized potential.

Learning analytics, by volume, timeliness, and composition, "expands the capacity and ability of organizations to make sense of complex environments" and promises to improve pedagogy, course design, student retention, and decision making by providing personalized feedback for users (Ali et al., 2012; Macfadyen & Dawson, 2012; Norris & Baer, 2013, p. 13). Slade and Prinsloo (2013) argue that "ignoring information that might actively help to pursue an institution's goals seems shortsighted to the extreme" (p. 14). This promise of learning analytics is alluring to higher education institutions, which are facing increasing pressure to provide evidence of student learning in an environment in which teaching pedagogical best practices are moving to an increasingly individualized and student-focused learning model and in which innovative technologies are allowing for greater mining of student data. Importantly, learning analytics also requires that student data that are often collected and housed across institutional silos be brought together in a data warehouse that allows for more sophisticated methods and a great understanding of student behavior and success. Taking the early success of the Purdue Course Signals Project as an example, data were brought together from their learning management system, grade book, student demographics, and transcripts to create the stoplight visualizations. On most college campuses, these data would reside separately in instructional technology, registrar, admissions, and institutional research offices. Within this context, learning and advising management systems, based on learning analytics, are being developed to better measure, analyze, report, and predict data related to student learning, retention, and completion. These learning analytics-informed systems have the potential to generate new insight into courses and student learning by creating responsive feedback mechanisms that can shape data-informed decision making as it relates to teaching, learning, and advising.

Status of Learning Analytics Research in Higher Education

Learning analytics is arguably just the latest educational technology purported to change or revolutionize educational practice. Just a few years ago, MOOCs took center stage in higher education news outlets on college campuses as the new premier tool that will forever alter the landscape of how colleges and universities offer courses. Selingo (2013) noted several ways that MOOCs could challenge the higher education enterprise by creating new modalities for online course delivery, new pathways for admission to highly selective universities, and new models for offering course credit; yet, even Selingo recognized that "none of these potential uses of the massive open courses are a panacea to the myriad of problems facing higher education. Nor can they fix the troubles facing any one college" (p. 93). We do not want to overstate learning analytics as a revolutionary tool that will forever change higher education as an industry; to do so would be to completely ignore the desires of students to maintain face-to-face faculty interactions and the established role that higher education plays in workforce development, economic growth, and community development (Arroway et al., 2016). In fact, more recent surveys of the usage of learning analytics in higher education found that application tended to stay in the areas of enrollment management and student success (Arroway et al., 2016). Yet, learning analytics does have potential to address a need for efficiencies in business operations and provide new methods and findings related to student success and learning.

Because learning analytics is an emergent field, there is a small, but growing field of literature related to use of learning analytics in higher education. These studies are often evaluative in nature and focus primarily on student and faculty experiences and interactions with learning analytics-based tools and their components. Examples of studies that have included research into student-perceived use and usefulness of these tools in reflecting on their coursework, tracking grades, building knowledge, and communicating with faculty and peers include Ali et al. (2012), Arnold and Pistilli (2012), Duval (2011), Kosba, Dimitrova, and Boyle (2005), Park and Jo (2015), Santos, Verbert, Govaerts, and Duval (2013), and Verbert et al. (2014). There have also been studies that have indicated that although learning analytics can be useful for student sensemaking, students will also act in opposition of intended outcomes (Jayaprakash, Moody, Lauría, Regan, & Baron, 2014; Park & Jo, 2015). Other studies on students suggest that data visualizations and interventions do have an impact on student behavior. Jayaprakash and colleagues (2014) found that students in the intervention groups of their quasiexperimental study of a learning analytics tool at Marist College withdrew at higher levels than the control groups. The unexpected withdrawal may be attributed in part to a lack of understanding of student needs on the part of developers or to misinterpretation of data or lack of trust in the data and tools on the part of students (Duval, 2011; Jayaprakash et al., 2014; Park & Jo, 2015; Verbert, Duval, Klerkx, Govaerts, & Santos, 2013; Verbert et al., 2014).

Studies on faculty and advisor use of learning analytics tools have focused mainly on feedback and data visualization, finding that these components, when done well, can help them identify potential areas for change or improvement in their pedagogy; however, poor feedback mechanisms and data visualization can also inhibit use (Ali et al., 2012; Lockyer, Heathcote, & Dawson, 2013). Although learning analytics feedback and visualizations can be useful, Hora, Bouwma-Gearheart, and Park (2014) found that even when data-driven decision making was understood as valuable, there are specific barriers and incentives in place related to the use of data by faculty, including a "lack of time due to workload; lack of expertise with educational data; perceived poor quality of data; course rotations," and incentives included "external accreditation policies; policies for course or departmental review; and availability of local experts" (pp.18–20). Further, Hora, Bouwma-Gearheart, and Park (2014) also note that institutional contexts constrain use of data in pedagogical decision making, as there is a lack of incentive, time, or high-quality data related to data-driven pedagogy.

Understanding organizational readiness and capacity to purchase, implement, and encourage widespread adoption of learning analytics in higher education institutions has been a relatively new focus for learning analytics researchers. Norris and Baer (2013)'s Organizational Capacity for Analytics Model outlines the capacity requirements related to broad adoption and use of these tools, including (a) technology infrastructure, (b) process and practices, (c) stakeholder skills and values, (d) culture, and (e) leadership (Norris & Baer, 2013, pp. 31–32). The Learning Analytics Readiness Instrument (LARI), developed by Arnold, Lonn, and Pistilli (2014), aligns with many of the components of the Norris and Baer (2013) model. Their study and corresponding instrument was developed to "fill the void in the literature regarding how an institution can proactively work to successfully implement learning analytics by understanding its own strengths and weaknesses" (Arnold et al., p. 4) and outlines five readiness factors used to evaluate institutional readiness for learning analytics: (a) ability, (b) data, (c) culture and process, (d) governance and infrastructure support, and (e) overall readiness (Arnold et al.).

The literature related to learning analytics provides insight into their use and development in higher education. However, learning analytics is evolving as quickly as they are being studied. Historically, many of the tools developed in the last decade have been course focused. Now, learning analytics is evolving to move beyond just predicting outcomes and suggesting actions for a particular course toward degree- or program-wide analysis (Grush, 2012). Newer learning analytics tools are mining student and institutional data to "develop strategies for instruction, advising, infrastructure, and resource allocation" based on predictive modeling (Rubel & Jones, 2016, p. 144). Learning analytics and predictive modeling are being used by the larger LMS corporate providers but national thought leaders are now suggesting a *next-generation digital learning environment* with cloud-based personalized integrated components that are more adaptable to individual learning environments and accessible to student with different needs (Siemens & Long, 2011). Next-generation learning analytics tools are in production that will personalize the student experience as students move through their coursework. Known as "intelligent curriculum," these tools will provide "each learner with resources, relevant to his or her profile, learning goals and the knowledge domain the learner is attempting to master" (Siemens & Long, 2011, p. 38; Ferguson, 2012). For students, the incorporation of predictive and personalized data into the feedback they receive via these new tools can "make education both personal and relevant and allow students to retain their own identities within the bigger system" (Slade & Prinsloo, 2013, p. 6).

Framework for Examining Learning Analytics in Higher Education

As we have stated, learning analytics as a field is new and emerging. The major association Learning Analytics & Knowledge has existed for less than 10 years; theoretical frameworks and research literature are just now beginning to emerge in large quantities. As with all new fields, learning analytics has drawn from a number of multidisciplinary trends and literatures to examine different facets of use, design, and implementation but has yet to bring together the complexity of external and internal organizational factors; faculty, advisor, and student motivation to engage in learning analytics adoption; and ethics and privacy concerns. This monograph draws from several areas of research in a comprehensive model of learning analytics in higher education. The purpose of this model is to identify the complex issues surrounding adoption of learning analytics in higher education that takes into account the organizational, technological, individual, and ethics literature.

Figure 1 represents five distinct areas of literature—organizational theory, technology alignment and adoption, faculty/advisor beliefs and behaviors, student use and action, and ethics and privacy—that affect the successful adoption and integration of learning analytics in higher education. Our model conceptualizes adoption of learning analytics in higher education as being done within the context of organizational factors (for example, infrastructure, change readiness, and so on) with ethics and privacy underlying all other areas, meaning ethics and privacy should be the guidepost for all decision making regarding learning analytics. For example, the use of student data from swiping identification cards at university events should be considered alongside data use policies, expectations of student privacy, and Family Educational Rights and Privacy Act (FERPA). Faculty and advisors are squarely in the context of the organizational factors highly influenced by institutional decision making, processes, and cultures. Faculty and advisors

FIGURE 1
Learning Analytics in Higher Education Adoption Model

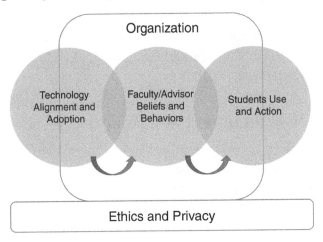

are using learning analytics based on organizational reward or awards, perceived institutional mission, and prior history and norms of data use. The technology and students are also influenced by the organizational factors but also exist outside of institutional influences. Technological advances occur in other fields (for example, bioinformatics), and students have prior experiences with technologies and data visualizations in other educational experiences. Next, we briefly summarize the literature in each area of Figure 1 with additional discussion in the second, third, and fourth chapters.

Organizational Theory

Although there are potential positives associated with the use of learning analytics tools in higher education, barriers and challenges exist that affect broad adoption and use. These barriers include a lack of interest or awareness, time, training, resources, incentives, institutional readiness, and institutional commitment, to name a few (Arnold et al., 2014; Austin, 2003; Bichsel, 2012; Brownell & Tanner, 2012; Fairweather, 2002, 2008; Macfadyen & Dawson, 2012; Norris & Baer, 2013; Tagg, 2012). Moreover, higher education institutions are notoriously slow in adopting new technologies, often lagging behind other industries, caused in part by complex and siloed organizational structures; competing institutional and individual demands and interests; lack of incentives to change behavior and practice; and disparate disciplinary influences (Amey, 1999; Austin, 2003, 2011; Austin & Sorcinelli, 2013; Bergquist, 1992; Birnbaum & Edelson, 1989; Brownell & Tanner, 2012; D'Avanzo, 2013; Eckel & Kezar, 2003; Kezar, 2001; Kezar & Eckel, 2002; Kezar & Lester, 2009; Sunal et al., 2001).

Technology Alignment and Adoption

A number of technology adoption models have developed over the years. Most of these models are informed by Rogers' (1995) foundational Innovation Diffusion Theory, which explored the role of the innovation, communication, social system(s), and time related to adoption. The Technology Acceptance Model (TAM; Davis, 1989) and the Universal Technology Adoption and Use Theory (UTAUT; Venkatesh, Morris, Davis, & Davis, 2003) focus on the attributes of individuals related to adoption of specific technologies, including perceptions, beliefs, attitudes, and so on (Davis, 1989; Straub, 2009; Venkatesh et al., 2003), and are particularly relevant for learning analytics adoption theories. Hall's (1979) Concerns Based Adoption Model is a P–20 education-based model for technology adoption that speaks to the specific concerns of faculty adopters. In 2007, Zellweger-Moser developed the Faculty Educational Technology Adoption Cycle (FETAC), which explicates the various considerations needed to encourage higher education faculty adoption of technology in their teaching practices. Common to all of these models are the decision-making points by individuals at the intersection of the organization and the technological innovation.

Faculty and Advisor Beliefs and Behaviors

Professional beliefs and their associated behaviors play a strong role in decisions by educators to adopt new practices, like technology, into their pedagogical practices (Ertmer, 2005; Hora & Holden, 2013; Liu, 2011; Rogers, 1995). Integral to decisions to adopt and integrate new technologies into practice are the professional beliefs that individuals hold (Hora & Holden,

2013; Kagan, 1992; Kim, Kim, Lee, Specter, & DeMeester, 2013; Liu, 2011; Ottenbreit-Leftwich, Glazewski, Newby, & Ertmer, 2010; Pajares, 1992). As Ertmer (2005, p. 29) notes, "The potential power of beliefs as influence on behavior is inherently related to the nature of beliefs" and technologies that align with individual value beliefs (belief that a technology has a value for individual pedagogical goals or practices), specifically, are more likely to be used by individuals (Hughes, 2005; Ottenbreit-Leftwich et al., 2010).

To encourage the adoption and use of technologies, like learning analytics, there must be a clear alignment between the technology and the user's belief system (Ertmer, 2005; Ertmer, Ottenbreit-Leftwich, Sadik, Sendurur, & Sendurur, 2012; Hora & Holden, 2013; Liu, 2011; Ottenbreit-Leftwich et al., 2010). For faculty, disciplinary difference and acculturation and professional identity can have a large impact on whether faculty adopt or reject new approaches to teaching pedagogy, course design, and student advising (Austin, 2011; Brownell & Tanner, 2012; D'Avanzo, 2013; Fairweather, 2008; Sunal et al., 2001). This is also true for advisors, who are, like faculty, socialized into professional norms around the purpose, scope, and delivery of their roles (Appleby, 2008; Crookston, 1994; Hagen & Jordan, 2008). Brownell and Tanner (2012) argue that disciplinary training and professional identity play a stronger role in acting as a barrier to change than the usual suspects of time and incentives.

Student Use and Action

The intended purpose of learning analytics is to help students through the use of personalized learning dashboards that visualize their data and provide feedback on their performance and potential. These dashboards are used not only to measure, analyze, predict, and improve student engagement, retention, and completion but also to alert students to their status in a course and provide major and career recommendations (Arnold & Pistilli, 2012; Baker & Yacef, 2009; Ben-Naim, Bain, & Marcus, 2009; Bichsel, 2012; Dahlstrom et al., 2014; Macfadyen & Dawson, 2012; Mazza & Dimitrova, 2007; Norris & Baer, 2013; Peña-Ayala, 2014). Although the evidence is mixed as to whether having learning analytics-based data improves individual student outcomes, students have reported that using these tools helps them reflect on coursework, track grades, and communicate with faculty and peers (Verbert et al., 2014).

However, although the data provided through these dashboards can be useful, they are also often provided without context or with unclear interventions (for example, emails or color-coded alerts) (Klein, Lester, Rangwala, & Johri, 2017). This lack of context makes it difficult for students to make sense of or to trust the data coming from learning analytics dashboards. Consequently, the intent of these tools (to improve student retention and completion) is often misaligned with subsequent student action (a student drops a course instead of following the intervention email encouraging him or her to meet with an advisor) (Jayaprakash et al., 2014). Because both understanding and trust are integral to user adoption of new technologies, context-free, unclear, or misaligned learning analytics data and interventions can hamper student use.

Ethics and Privacy

Although learning analytics has evolved over the last decade to be an increasingly important force in higher education data-driven decision making, researchers are only now just beginning to understand ethics, power, and privacy implications related to this new technology. Although relatively scant, recent scholarly papers and studies have focused on issues of surveillance and power (Andrejevic, 2011; Lyon, 2007), privacy (Coll, Glassey, & Balleys, 2011; Petersen, 2012; Prinsloo & Slade, 2013, 2015; Slade & Prinsloo, 2013), and ethics (Pardo & Siemens, 2015; Slade & Prinsloo, 2013). Among the work of these papers is to create shared and agreed-upon definitions of ethics and privacy, to outline the various legal frameworks that are connected to ethical use of data and privacy protection, and to begin to establish codes of practice that learning analytics developers and higher education administrators can follow in the design, development, implementation, and ongoing maintenance of these tools. Given the important of protecting user data, ethics and privacy investigation as it relates to learning analytics is an important arena for future work.

Outline of the Monograph

This book is organized around five separate chapters that comprehensively review the status of learning analytics in higher education. The second chapter takes a deeper dive into the model of learning analytics in higher education with a focus on organizational studies, technology adoption, and faculty pedagogy change to offer insights into the complexities of learning analytics adoption. We explore themes related to the role of organizational environment (including resources, structure, culture, and incentives) and technological capacity and capabilities (including functionality, usefulness, and alignment with user needs). The third chapter explores individual decision making and the relationship between faculty identity and beliefs as well as student use. Within this chapter, we discuss individual factors (including beliefs, values, interests, and efficacy) related to learning analytics-based technologies and other educational technology tools.

The fourth chapter reviews the ethical considerations related to use of learning analytics in higher education. Specifically, we explore the challenges of algorithmic bias in creating analytics-based technologies, including the choices related to including specific data points in learning analytics algorithms (especially demographic-based data) and the use of those data to predict student outcomes. Further, we review the privacy concerns related to collection, use, and ownership of student faculty and staff data and issues related to individual agency in an age of educational data mining. The fifth and final chapter summarizes the book and includes practical implications and future suggestions for research, based on research and literature related to learning analytics in higher education.

How Organizational Context and Capacity and Technological Alignment Affect Learning Analytics Adoption

Angela walks into the student union building and is immediately surprised by the balloons, people handing out buttons, and music. Immediately, a button is put in her hand that reads, "ENGAGE: Tools to support your learning!" Quickly, Angela remembers that series of emails sent out announcing that March 1 is the university-designated day to celebrate and advertise a new learning analytics tool purchased by the university to support student learning. In her role as an assistant professor, Angela has been asked to use and encourage students to use ENGAGE. Availability of new tools is common at Mid-Atlantic University but this one does seem to integrate a lot of data and have some customization and snazzy visualizations. Angela will give it a try this afternoon. Yet, there are some immediate concerns: Does the university really have clean and verifiable data on students as it suggests? Do the tools really help with student success? Are there staff to support the tool given how complex it appears? Will advisors, faculty, and students really use it? And, will it just complicate my job further as opposed to helping with efficiency? Is Mid-Atlantic really ready for learning analytics tools?

Matt receives an email from central administration at Mid-Atlantic University introducing a new campaign—ENGAGE— with associated learning analytic tools to support academic advising and student course selection among other options for faculty. The email asks academic advisors like Matt to log on to the new tool and use it during student advising sessions. Matt is incredulous and responds with an audible sigh. In his estimation, this is the third new tool purchased in the last 5 years; the other two were discontinued because they lacked use and were inaccurate. Matt logs on, creates a new account, and begins to explore the tool; he finds that the data visualization showing students' degree progress helpful as an easy and quick reference. However, he immediately finds inaccuracies mostly related to the many exceptions (for example, course substitution and community college transfer student credit application) for courses and credits. Matt works in a complex degree plan academic program. Matt immediately goes back to his old spreadsheet system that although not technologically advanced is accurate and trustworthy. Yet again, the institution would have been advised to consult with advisors to ensure that users were getting what they needed out of a new tool.

Introduction

As discussed in the first chapter, learning analytics tools have great potential to affect higher education institutions and its members. Many of these potential impacts are positive and range from illuminating patterns in student course taking and performance, providing feedback mechanisms for faculty to improve pedagogy, and allowing faculty and advisors to have a more holistic view of their students as a means to improve their experience and classroom performance. Despite the potential, learning analytics exists within specific contexts that affect the efficacy and impacts of these tools. Specifically, there are unique organizational, technological, and pedagogical environments to higher education that create both barriers and opportunities for successful implementation and subsequent adoption of learning analytics by faculty, advisors, and students. Faculty members like Angela and advisors like Matt are the frontline users of these tools, dealing directly with the opportunities and barriers that learning analytics bring. The purpose of this chapter and the next is to bring together the literature on organizational studies, technology adoption, and faculty pedagogy to conceptualize a framework to implement and research learning analytics in higher education. We proposed and introduced in the first chapter a multilayer framework that accounts for organizational external influences that often catalyze the need for more efficient and sophisticated automated tools, factors that influence faculty behavioral change with an emphasis on adoption of technology and pedagogy, and how the state of the technology affects the ability to successfully implement learning analytics for change. We also include the research on college student success, specifically retention as many of the learning analytics tools are attempting to automate and support institutional efforts to increase student retention, coupled with student-focused learning analytics literature. We recognize that the interventions of learning analytics will change over time but do maintain that student retention and completion are hallmarks of the college mission and core to the ultimate purpose of these tools.

Throughout this chapter and the next, we draw on the existing theoretical and empirical work to review each area of the framework as well as studies we conducted from a National Science Foundation (NSF) project on learning analytics in higher education to illustrate the arguments. The NSF project is an exploratory research project focused on the creation of a new learning analytics teaching and advising tool. A goal of this project is to identify opportunities and challenges related to adoption of learning analytics tools by higher education institutions and its members, primarily faculty, advisors, and students. Via this work, which has focused on these complex contexts of learning analytics technology implementation by institutions and individual decisions to adopt these tools, we have pulled from a number of frameworks that have helped us situate our findings. These frameworks and their associated literature span organizational, technological, and pedagogical contexts. The organizational factors that create barriers and opportunities for learning analytics implementation and adoption in higher education are rooted in issues of institutional structures, commitment, resources, readiness, capacity, and a lack of incentives and rewards (Arnold et al., 2014; Austin, 2011; Bichsel, 2012; Kezar & Lester, 2009; Macfadyen & Dawson, 2012; Norris & Baer, 2013). Lack of proper infrastructure, resources, personnel, and a culture of learning analytics readiness can negatively affect deployment of these tools on campus (Arnold, Lonn, & Pistilli, 2014; Norris & Baer, 2013). Implementation of learning analytics also requires attention to a host of technological factors to include provision of data, technical data analytics expertise, cross-organization collaboration, leadership, and attention to organizational climate (Arnold et al., 2014; Bichsel, 2012; Ferguson, 2012; Klein, Lester, Rangwala, & Johri, in press; Norris & Baer, 2013).

Technological constraints exist on multiple levels including a lack of appropriate infrastructure, adequate support and technical staff, adequate levels of data, and lack of alignment and integration of learning analytics tool data into already existing technologies (Arnold et al., 2014; Bichsel, 2012; Klein et al., in press; Norris & Baer, 2013). Individual decisions by faculty and advisors to use or refuse learning analytics tools hinge on awareness, interest, time, training, disciplinary socialization and personal beliefs, and trust (Amey, 1999; Austin, 2003, 2011; Bichsel, 2012; Dahlstrom et al., 2014; Fairweather, 2008; Hora & Holden, 2013; Klein et al., in press, 2016b; Norris & Baer, 2013). Students face similar decision points based on trust, alignment, understanding, and usefulness of the data they use and interpret (Arnold & Pistilli, 2012; Park & Jo, 2015, Verbert et al., 2013, 2014). Clearly, the context in which learning analytics in higher education exists and is implemented and adopted is incredibly complex. This complexity must be understood in order to both maximize the potential of learning analytics in higher education and ensure learning analytics' relevance to organizations and individuals.

It is important to note that given the emergent and rapidly evolving nature of the literature associated with learning analytics use in higher education, specifically, none of the frameworks reviewed here are specific to learning analytics in higher education. Rather they are pulled from various organizational, technological, and pedagogical theoretical models that have been associated with technology and higher education and that we argue can be extended to consider learning analytics use in higher education. What follows is a review of those frameworks coupled with relevant literature from the fields of learning analytics, organizational theory, and higher education to provide additional context as it relates to learning analytics use in higher education.

The focus of this chapter is on the various theoretical frameworks and literature associated with organizational and technological aspects of learning analytics implementation and adoption in higher education institutions. We begin with an overview of a multilevel organizational model for individual decision making, which includes individual contexts and institutional contexts and levers. This overview is followed by a brief review of the literature on organizational change, institutional logics, and capacity and readiness related to learning analytics tools in higher education. The chapter concludes with an overview of technological aspects of learning analytics tools and individual decision making, including a review of innovation adoption and tool alignment. This investigation of individual decision making within the organizational context continues in the third chapter, which focuses on the faculty and advisor pedagogical decision making and introduces student decision making related to learning analytics tool use. Underpinning the framework of learning analytics in higher education is ethics and privacy. Given the complexity of ethical principles and privacy concerns, the fourth chapter is dedicated to this topic.

An Organizational Model for Individual Decision Making

Among the most useful frameworks for understanding the complexities related to individual decision making within higher education organizational structures is Austin's (2011) Systems Model for Understanding Faculty Teaching Decisions. Although originally intended to model the relationships between various organizational components, contexts, and faculty decision making related to undergraduate science pedagogy, the model nicely acknowledges the unique nature of higher education organizations and the complexities associated with individual decision making within that system. Further, we have extended this model to include professional advising staff, as advising is regarded as a form of teaching (Appleby, 2008; Crookston, 1994; Hagen & Jordan, 2008), and advisors are similarly affected by the various organizational components covered in the Austin model and face similar issues related to technology adoption as faculty do.

Austin's (2011) nested systems model explains the barriers and incentives related to faculty pedagogical change, specifically: "(1) individual faculty members bring values, backgrounds, abilities, and aspirations to their teaching that relate to the decisions they make; (2) teaching occurs within organizational contexts internal and external to the higher education organization that influence teaching-related decisions; and (3) several organizational levers are particularly relevant to faculty members' decisions about their teaching" (p. 4). These three areas—the factors (individual variables) that each faculty member possesses; levels (context and cultures) that comprise the university, both within and beyond its boundaries; and the levers (rewards, workload, and so on) within higher education organizations—influence how and to what degree faculty will adopt new behaviors and ways of being and create incentives and barriers to change (Austin, 2011). For faculty and advisors, like Angela and Matt in the opening vignette, who they are, how they have been socialized, and the environment in which they work informs their decision making, which includes their decisions whether and how to use learning analytics tools.

Individual Factors

At the core of Austin's (2011) model are individuals—the work they do and the choices they make—and how individual factors, like "values, backgrounds, abilities and aspirations to their teaching" affect their approach to pedagogical decision making (p. 4). Austin argues that understanding "the individual variables that affect faculty members approaches to their work is an important part of understanding the way they teach" (p. 5). Among the "key variables" that influence pedagogical perspectives and behavior are prior experience, doctoral socialization, discipline, career stage, appointment type, and motivation (Austin, 2011, p. 5). For Angela and Matt, how they were socialized into their fields will affect whether or not they are motivated to incorporate learning analytics tools into their practice.

Institutional Levels

The external, institutional, and departmental environments comprise the "levels of the system that influence faculty work in implicit and explicit ways" (Austin, 2011, p. 3). Austin (2011, 2003) and Austin and Sorcinelli (2013) argue that these environmental pressures are shaping faculty roles in new ways, a perspective that is shared by Amey (1999), who also argues that the shifting structure of higher education is also having an effect on faculty, who are increasingly being called on to make teaching and student outcomes a priority. Environmental factors include the increasing accountability demands, the "rise of new technologies, increasing diversity of students, new educational institutions [and subsequent competition], greater emphasis on learning outcomes, a postmodern approach to knowledge; and changes in the demographics of faculty" (Austin, 2003, p. 123; Kezar & Lester, 2009). The issues related to faculty identity, beliefs, and behaviors are explored more fully in the third chapter.

Further, Austin and Sorcinelli (2013) speak to the "integration of technology into teaching, learning and research" as a driver in faculty pedagogical change (p. 89). Although not explicitly highlighted in Austin's (2011) model, technological innovation as a promised salve for student retention is a key part of the external environmental level affecting adoption of technologically innovative practices on campus. When combined with external levels of pressure by government and governance for increased student engagement and internal institution-level reaction to that pressure, technology creates an additional level of decision-making consideration for faculty and advising staff in approaching their work.

These environmental pressures work at numerous levels to act as barriers in adoption of new ways of being. Locke (1995) states that these barriers can include issues of prestige, institutional inertia, competing demands and pressures, and incentives as they relate to faculty behavior change (Locke, 1995, pp. 516–519). At the administrative level, decisions to purchase tools like ENGAGE to respond to the environmental pressures institutions are facing affect faculty and advisors. The introduction of these tools create decision points for faculty and advisors, like Angela and Matt, who must decide whether or not to use these tools and to what extent.

Institutional Levers

The third part of Austin's (2011) model are the "components within the organizational environment can operate as barriers to change or can serve as 'levers' to promote change in faculty behaviors" (p. 11). Austin notes the importance of rewards systems in order to shift the value of teaching toward a level more equitable to research (2011). Both Austin (2011) and Fairweather (2008) note that rewards and revised work allocation are more likely levers to engender adoption of new pedagogical practice than is evidence-based information. Thus, in order to boost the chances that pedagogical change will take place, institutional components must make pedagogical shifts easy for faculty to learn, use, and incorporate, so as to not take up valuable time. Incorporating leadership at various levels of the institution who "encourages, supports, and rewards teaching innovations that support student learning" also is noted by Austin as a useful strategy in resocializing faculty toward new ways of thinking about their pedagogical approaches, as is use of meaningful professional development opportunities that are viewed as an opportunity rather than a burden (p. 15).

Fairweather (2008) concurs with Austin (2011) on a multipronged approach to leveraging change. He also suggests changes to motivate faculty behavioral shifts, including "developing distinct models for implementation, dissemination and institutionalization; effective use of teaching and learning centers; external networks of like-minded colleagues; leveraging of professional societies; and using senior faculty to incorporate graduate students and new faculty" into an appreciation of pedagogical changes (pp. 26–27). Like Fairweather and Austin, Dusick's (1998) study of faculty adoption of computing technology in education states the necessity for a comprehensive approach to providing incentives for change. He divides factors for change into three areas: environmental, behavioral, and personal. Among the factors influencing positive choice behaviors in this study were environmental (supportive administration, available training, revised pedagogy, funding, release time, and tech-friendly job titles); behavioral (time commitment, personal risk, and willingness to participate in training); and personal (attitude, anxiety, self-efficacy, competency, beliefs, perceptions of relevance, and knowledge) (Dusick, 1998, p. 133). Both the Austin's (2011) and Dusick's (1998) models conceptualize a multilevel approach to pedagogy change focusing on individual behaviors, including perspectives and experiences, and on environmental influences, including the organizational and disciplinary contexts.

The organizational, technological, and pedagogical issues associated with learning analytics use in higher education can be explained at various levels of Austin's model. Specific incentives and barriers to broad adoption and integration of institutionally supported learning analytics tools are found at the various context levels of Austin's (2011) model. The siloed environments of most higher education institutions are "comprised of multiple contexts and cultures within which individual faculty members work" and are composed of various colleges, departments, and disciplines, with varying resources, decisions, and power, which create a multilevel system that "influence[s] faculty work in implicit and explicit ways" (p. 3). In the Austin's model, the multilevel internal systems of higher education institutions and the environments in which those institutions exist influence decisions by faculty to adopt pedagogical innovations. Moreover, Austin (2011) argues that rewards, professional development, and strategic leadership present within the contexts of higher education can be leveraged to promote individual decision making and pedagogical change. Although Austin's model does not specifically address the integration of learning analytics into pedagogical practice within the context of higher education organizations, technology integration is an important component of pedagogical change that is reliant on organizational context (Austin & Sorcinelli, 2013).

Organizational Context

For higher education, as a professional bureaucracy with multiple and often siloed organizational subcomponents, the introduction and implementation of any innovation are likely to take time (Austin, 2011; Kezar, 2001). Research on organizational change in higher education often notes that collaboration and coordination are necessary when working across units and colleges that have different structures, policies, and cultural and social norms (Kezar & Lester, 2009). This time lag exists with all new technologies but is often compounded in higher education institutions, in part because they can lack the capacity, resources, and readiness to create a technological context that can support the needs of users. As a result, broad adoption of these technologies is often hampered (Arnold et al., 2014; Bichsel, 2012; Macfadyen & Dawson, 2012; Norris & Baer, 2013). Even when readiness and capacity levels are optimal, traditional top-down implementation can hinder institution-wide adoption of new technologies especially in fragmented higher education institutions (Baltaci-Goktalay & Ocak, 2006). Moreover, institutional logics play a role in shaping individual perceptions and decision making that can affect the pace and direction of organizational change (Bastedo, 2009). Ultimately, the issue of organizational capacity and readiness can affect institutional use and perceived effectiveness of educational technology tools (learning analytics based or otherwise) in decision-making and planning processes (Arnold et al., 2014; Macfadyen & Dawson, 2012; Norris & Baer, 2013). Thus, it is important to understand the complexities of organizational change, the institutional logics from which decisions to implement and adopt tools are made, and the capacity and resource capabilities of higher education institutions.

Organizational Change

Organizational change on college campuses is rife with difficulties. Large, bureaucratic, and loosely coupled structures with longstanding cultural norms often thwart change efforts and lead to the perception that higher education institutions rarely change or do so only after decades of effort. Yet, change does happen on college campuses readily with many models that identify the various concerns, approaches, and strategies to promote successful change (Kezar, 2014). In her 2014 book, Kezar, taking into account institutional cultural and contextual influences, provides a series of steps toward change that account for the content, scope, levels, focus, forces, and sources of change. For example, levels of change are important—do institutions or change agents want to engage in more locally based first-order change or more diffuse second-order change? Other considerations are the level of the organization (in other words, department, college, or university) and who or what is driving the change, such as a change in student demographics, research on a need to promote active learning in pedagogy, or decreases in state appropriations.

This model is affected by the socially constructed reality of individuals in the organization including those who are working toward change (for example, what they frame as problems that need to be addressed) and by accounting for how constituents in the college perceive of the change initiative (for example, what they see as the way to address the problem to change). In the case of learning analytics often the issue to address is low percentages of students who complete college. The rationale for the learning analytics tools is that they can help to identify those students who are in danger of or predicted to drop out of college. Early warning systems and the like have been developed and integrated to identify and intervene with these students. Student retention is the problem, and learning analytics tools are a strategy to address the problem. In our work, the definition and meaning of the problem may be shared across constituents but the use of learning analytics as a strategy is not (Klein, Lester, Rangwala, & Johri, in press, 2016a, 2016b). Advisors and faculty do not view an online tool as the intervention but more hands-on advising and mentoring as the effective practice. The lack of alignment can thwart the effective use of learning analytics tools making organizational considerations essential. For Matt, ENGAGE, although well intentioned, was an ill-devised tool for his specific needs and he found that his socialized face-to-face advising practices were more effective and not always enhanced by use of the tool. This disconnection between intended and actual use may be rooted in a difference in logics between learning analytics vendors, higher education administrators, and the faculty and advisors who use these tools.

Institutional Logics

Institutional logics play an important role in limiting or promoting organizational change. When logics align with new innovations, they can prime organizations for change, like the implementation and adoption of learning analytics tools. However, when logics are misaligned, change can be hindered. Institutional logics are "the complicated, experientially constructed thereby contingent set of rules, premiums, and sanctions that men and women in particular contexts create and recreate in such a way that their behavior and accompanying perspectives are to some extent regularized and predictable. Put succinctly, institutional logics is the way a social world works" (Jackall,

1988, p. 112). Institutional logics include culturally held values, assumptions, beliefs, and the "rules" that "construct and reconstruct" organizational realities (Friedland & Alford, 1991; Thornton & Ocasio, 2008, p. 101; Thornton & Ocasio, 1999). Further, these logics exist on multiple environmental levels (societal, market, and so on) and organizational levels (overarching institution, subunits, and so on) and consists of the "organizing principles that organizations use when making decisions within a specific arena" (Bastedo, 2009, p. 211; Friedland & Alford, 1991, p. 248; Thornton & Ocasio, 2008).

The decision making that emerges from institutional logics is often a result of institutional demands, which, like logics, exist both externally and internally and at multiple levels, like those in Austin's (2011) model. Institutional demands are the organizational pressures that "emanate from the organization's broader regulatory, social and cultural environments," and that "permeate organizational boundaries" (Pache & Santos, 2010, p. 11). These pressures manifest from the actions of outside actors, like funders, regulators, and other stakeholders, and from the internal isomorphic tendencies of organizations through hiring practices, cultural norms, and socialization (Pache & Santos). Further, in fragmented institutions like higher education organizations, these demands are often met with complex and uneven organizational responses by organizational units and individuals, both internal and external to the institution (Pache & Santos). As such, institutional demands and institutional logics intersect at the point when individuals decide whether or not to take action that is influenced by how institutions have articulated and made meaning of how an institution should act on those influence. As logics relate to learning analytics, there is a tension between tools that are developed by vendors but used by higher education institution members, who are operating from different perspectives and from different logics that inform issues related to the goals and outcomes of learning analytics use. In addition, how an institution frames its needs, such as needing to increase student retention and graduation rate, influences what tools are developed and how they are marketed. This articulation is often occurring at the upper administration level without concern for the needs of users—advisors, faculty, and students, for example. Within this symbiotic relationship, "embedded agency" of individuals is both promoted and constrained by overarching logics (Giddens, 1984; Seo & Creed, 2002; Thornton & Ocasio, 2008), whereas institutional logics are simultaneously "constructed by the social actions of individuals" (Berger & Luckmann, 1966; Thornton & Ocasio, 2008, p. 104). Both Matt and Angela used their agency to decide whether and how they would use the ENGAGE tool. How agency is expressed through individual beliefs, behaviors, and actions and how those beliefs, behaviors, and actions affect learning analytics adoption are explored more fully in the third chapter.

Organizational Readiness and Capacity

In addition to change and logics, organizational capacity and readiness to implement learning analytics place a large role in their success in higher education institutions. In the opening vignette, Angela's questions were tied to the issue of organizational capacity and readiness, and they speak to the importance of users understanding what resources are available to implement and support learning analytics tools. There are only a few studies that have focused on these aspects of organizational support for learning analytics implementation. Norris and Baer (2013) provide insight into the various capacity issues related to learning analytics implementation and adoption through their Organizational Capacity for Analytics Model, and Arnold et al.'s (2014) Learning Analytics Readiness Instrument was developed to better understand components of institutional readiness for these technologies.

Norris and Baer (2013) explore the necessary components related to organizational capacity via analysis of current learning analytics use in higher education and the organizational capacity necessary to improve adoption and use of learning analytics in higher education institutions. Their model, based on data from 40 higher education institutions and 20 analytics vendors, explores the interconnected "five factors for building organizational capacity" for learning analytics in higher education: technology infrastructure (including the "technology environment for individual institutions" that allows improved decision making through use of learning analytics tools); process and practices (including policies that are "embedded in the fabric of institutions and used effectively by all faculty, staff and students"); stakeholder skills and values (including the "willingness" to incorporate use of tools into daily practice); culture and behaviors (that are focused on performance as a result of analytics feedback); and leadership (that provides "long-term commitment to launching, resourcing, scaling, and sustaining" analytics adoption) (Norris & Baer, pp. 31–32).

Like Norris and Baer's (2013) model, the Learning Analytics Readiness Instrument created by Arnold et al. (2014) was developed to "fill the void in the literature regarding how an institution can proactively work to successfully implement learning analytics by understanding its own strengths and weaknesses" (p. 4). Constructed through qualitative data collection from 33 universities successfully using learning analytics on their campuses, the LARI includes 5 readiness factors: ability (of staff and faculty to develop and use these systems); data (type and volume of data collected); culture and process (related to "institutional norms" of use and sharing of data); governance and infrastructure support (including investment, policies, and oversight); and overall readiness (including faculty acceptance and support and institutional resources) (Arnold et al., 2014).

Though not extensive, the data from Arnold et al. (2014) and from Norris and Baer (2013) provide an understanding of the interconnected institutional factors related to readiness for adoption of learning analytics tools by higher education institutions. Combining the perspective on institutional readiness and capacity for technology innovations, with the organizational systems model offered by Austin and with the literature on organizational change and institutional logics, provides a strong frame for understanding the interplay between the institution and individual in adoption of learning tools in higher education.

Our work has extended these models by underscoring the importance of inclusion and transparency as trust-building organizational levers that can encourage adoption of learning analytics tools (Klein et al., in press). Trust building is a foundational activity that is especially important when implementing learning analytics tools, which are often less trusted because of concerns related to bias and predictive outcomes. Building user support for learning tools cannot be a top-down process. Rather it must be an inclusive process that incorporates user needs, roles, and voices throughout the process of purchase, implementation, and adoption of learning analytics tools.

Although answering questions of capacity and readiness can help users like Angela better understand how tools can be used, learning analytics can be effective only when the technological components of the tools align with users' needs.

Technology Adoption and Alignment

Like organizational readiness and capacity, issues related to the technological aspects of innovations, like learning analytics tools, affect their adoption and use. Successful adoption of technologies is often dependent upon the use, efficacy and efficiency of these tools. Even when these standards are met, technologies must also be aligned and relevant to the work users do to encourage integration into regular practice.

Technology Adoption Models

Technological innovations can often change the ways in which individuals approach their work once a technology is adopted. However, there is often a time lag between the development (or supply) of a technology and its adoption (or demand), which is affected by environmental contexts and individual factors (Balcer & Lippman, 1984). Time lags exist in the space between the "invention of a paradigm-altering technology from its everyday use" and is often affected by environmental context, organizational culture and individual perspectives, behaviors, and attitudes (Privateer, 1999, p. 1; Rogers, 1995; Straub, 2009). This lag is present in the higher education environment, as new technologies, like learning analytics, have been introduced over the past decade.

Traditional Adoption Models

A number of technology adoption models have historically been used to explicate the process in which users decide to integrate a new technology into their practices. Among the most well known are the Technology Acceptance Model (TAM; Davis, 1989) and the Universal Technology Adoption and Use Theory (UTAUT; Venkatesh et al., 2003). Informed by Rogers' (1995) Innovation Diffusion Theory, which explored the role of the innovation, communication, social system(s), and time related to adoption, the TAM and UTAUT focus on the individual perceptions, beliefs, and attitudes related to technology adoption (Davis, 1989; Straub, 2009; Venkatesh et al., 2003). In the TAM model, users' attitudes, behaviors, and ultimate decisions to adopt a technology are influenced by the "perceived usefulness" and "perceived ease of use" of that technology (Davis, 1989). Although the focus of the TAM in on individual perceptions related to technology adoption, the UTAUT accounts for the expectations, influences, and conditions that facilitate adoption. The UTAUT argues that the following factors influence adoption levels: (a) performance expectancy (level of belief in system ability to aid in attainment of professional goals); (b) effort expectancy (level of perceived system ease of use); (c) social influence (level of perceived importance of adoption by important others); and (d) facilitating conditions (level of belief that "an organizational and technical infrastructure exists to support the system") (Straub, 2009; Venkatesh et al., 2003, p. 453). Although the TAM and UTAUT provide a useful explanation of the individual components related to adoption of technologies, they are not specific to the unique context of educational environments.

Education-Focused Adoption Models

Among the adoption models specific to education, the Concerns-Based Adoption Model (CBAM) and the Faculty Educational Technology Adoption Cycle are among the most useful in communicating the specific circumstances related to faculty adoption of technology. The CBAM (Hall, 1979) was created to understand how faculty, in all levels of education, choose to adopt technology into their pedagogical practice, at all levels of use. The CBAM focuses on "motivations, perceptions, attitudes and feelings" of faculty within the unique context of educational institutions and is composed of six stages of concern: Awareness (level of understanding/concern about the innovation); Informational ("general awareness of the innovation . . . general characteristics, effects and requirements for use"); Personal (level of understanding/concern related to innovation's requirements, from an individual perspective—including pulls on time, potential rewards, or conflicts; Management (perceptions/concerns related to usefulness, efficacy, and efficiency of the tool); Consequence (concerns about an innovation's relevance to practice and impact on students); Collaboration (issues related to "coordination and collaboration" with colleagues, students, administration, and so on); and Refocusing (exploration of the "universal benefits" of the innovation and how that innovation can improved based on that exploration) (Hall, 1979, p. 8). Hall argues that each of these stages of concern is associated with corresponding levels of adoption. The higher the level of concern or the lower their awareness or knowledge is related to that technology, the less likely a faculty member is to adopt a technology. To allay concern and improve adoption rates, Hall encourages change agents to make relevant connections between the innovation and faculty needs.

Similarly, Zellweger-Moser's FETAC outlines the various considerations needed to encourage faculty adoption of technology in their teaching practices. The model is designed specifically to address the challenge of integrating new technologies into complex higher education infrastructures within a professional bureaucracy composed of faculty with varying values, goals, trust levels, and available time to adopt new teaching technologies (Zellweger-Moser, 2007a, 2007b). The model is based on "a circuit of faculty behavior activities which are influenced by several outside factors and conditions" (Zellweger-Moser, 2007a, p. 66). These behaviors include time commitment, competence development, course design, teaching/learning experience, and reflection. Each of these behaviors is influenced by environmental factors. Time commitment is shaped by individual characteristics (values, "innovativeness," experiences, and goals) and an incentive structure; competence development (via training) and educational technology course design is influenced by resources and support; the teaching/learning experience is affected by trustworthy infrastructures (or lack thereof); and reflection is informed by peer and student feedback (Zellweger-Moser, 2007a, p. 66). The model is iterative and each cycle informs subsequent cycles.

According to Moser (2007), time is integral to the model, as "time is a scarce resource" for faculty. Incorporating educational technologies requires a commitment of time that is supported both extrinsically, via the organization, and intrinsically, via individual interest (Zellweger-Moser, 2007a, 2007b). Connected to time is the need to have well-designed training and trustworthy infrastructures to help ensure that users understand how to use new technologies, but those technologies are also appropriately supported. When technology does not work, the teaching and learning experience is affected, which leads to a mistrust of the technology and a negative assessment of its usefulness. News of these negative experiences can "travel fast and influence the opinions of the larger community" (Zellweger-Moser, 2007a, p. 67) and can affect the amount of time faculty are willing to give an innovation. Thus, the cycle begins, again, but with potentially diminished time commitment by faculty users.

The implications of the various adoption models presented here are that perceptions of usefulness and ease of use, expectations related to use of technologies, concerns related to those technologies, and the required time commitment and trustworthy infrastructures are important factors affecting faculty assessment and ultimately use of learning analytics tools. Another important factor, based on literature related to adoption of learning analytics, specifically, is the alignment of learning analytics tools to users' needs. When learning analytics tools are poorly aligned to users' needs or are not trustworthy, as is the case of Matt's experience with the ENGAGE tool, users are more likely to marginalize or reject learning analytics tools.

Technology Alignment

Unique technological challenges are associated with the introduction of learning analytics into higher education. There is no doubt that higher education is moving toward more data-informed decision making and much of the future of that decision making will rely on adoption of learning analytics (Bichsel, 2012; Dahlstrom et al., 2014; Norris & Baer, 2013), but technological constraints are also present in the tools themselves that inhibit widespread adoption and use. These constraints exist as a result of a lack of technological alignment between learning analytics and the relevancy of these tools to its users. Although the bulk of literature has revolved around faculty and advisor adoption of these tools (as students are often required to use these tools as part of their coursework and course management), research for all users indicates that the ability to gain trusted, accurate, visually understandable, and relevant data that align with their needs are key factors related to adoption (Ali et al.,

2012; Austin, 2011; Dawson, McWilliam, & Tan, 2008; Klein et al., in press, 2016a, 2017).

Of the studies focusing particularly on faculty use of learning analytics tools, the majority of work focuses on the barriers to adoption of these tools, namely: lack of clear, relevant, timely, or trustworthy data. Ali et al. (2012) offer insight into the technological barriers and incentives for faculty integration of learning analytics technology into their teaching. They designed a learning analytics feedback tool related to teaching and learning and asked study participants about the tool's value (Ali et al., 2012). Faculty valued the data and visualizations provided by the tool and reported useful ways of using the tool to enhance their teaching but only if the data and visualizations were relevant, understandable, and easy to use (Ali et al., 2012). Dawson et al. (2008) also noted the importance of data visualization for faculty and advisor users as poor visualizations have the potential to "constrain staff understanding of the linkage between student online interactions and implemented pedagogical approach" (p. 228).

Lockyer et al. (2013) argue that this linkage is necessary for faculty use of learning analytics systems. To be useful and effective, learning analytics need to connect the divide between education and technology and to provide "just-in-time, useful and context-sensitive feedback on how well the learning design is meeting educational outcomes" (Lockyer, Heathcote, & Dawson, p. 1446). However, when that connection is absent or when technologies do not meet expectations, barriers are erected by users that usually center around trust related to the data that are being conveyed or a lack of technological expertise by users that inhibit their action (Hora et al., 2014). Dahlstrom et al. (2014) found that barriers can also center around aspects of technologies that do not align with users' needs or experiences, finding that although "faculty value the LMS as an enhancement to their teaching and learning experiences . . . relatively few use the advanced features and even fewer use these systems to their fullest capacity" (p. 10). This is owing, in part, to a feeling that tools are not personalized, "bloated (= zillions of features we do not need), badly designed (features we need are not streamlined, easy to use, intuitive), and cumbersome [system]" (Dahlstrom et al., 2014, p. 10). Our work aligns with much of the previous literature on the technological barriers and incentives to technology adoption (Klein et al., 2016a). The faculty and advisors whom we interviewed reported that a lack of integration and flexibility was a chief complaint. Without integrated, flexible systems, learning analytics tools were not only less likely to be used but were more likely to be viewed as inaccurate or untrustworthy.

Conclusion and Future Work

The organizational and technological contexts related to learning analytics have an impact on users' decision-making processes. Pulling from the various organizational theories related to pedagogical decision making, change, and logic; from the various technology adoption theories; and from work on learning analytics capacity and readiness allows an understanding of how faculty and advisors, like Angela and Matt choose to interact with learning analytics tools. However, our understanding is still fairly rudimentary, because more work needs to be done in this area. Specifically, given the power and potential of learning analytics, future work should seek to understand what organizational factors, including logic, readiness, and capacity and technological adoption and alignment, are influencing and can be influenced by the use of learning analytics in higher education.

This chapter focused primarily on organizational and technological aspects of learning analytics adoption by users. Yet, faculty and advisor pedagogical perspective also plays a large role in decisions to use learning analytics. Issues of professionalization and socialization and their impact on beliefs, behaviors, and decision making related to learning analytics adoption are explored more fully in the third chapter, as is a review of student sensemaking and actions related to learning analytics dashboard data and interventions.

Faculty, Advisor, and Student Decision Making Related to Use of Learning Analytics Data and Tools

Alicia has just started her sophomore year and is excited and a little daunted by her load of courses. She is taking 16 credits this semester, two general education requirements and three courses in her major, computer science. Although she knows the semester will be challenging, she is confident in her ability to succeed because she is a strong student, having done well in both high school and in her first-year courses at her university. Moreover, because she is the first in her family to go to college and has received a scholarship that has covered her tuition she feels a strong sense of responsibility in succeeding. Six weeks into the new semester, Alicia receives an alert through her schools early warning system. The system was purchased by her university as a new technology to help inform students of their progress. Alicia is a part of a pilot group of students whose individual and course data, through the school's learning management system, are mined to predict likelihood of successful course completion. Alicia was automatically selected to be a part of this pilot when she signed up for her sophomore semester courses. Alicia is aware of this system and has received some basic information on the purpose of the system. Alicia feels confident that, despite one low quiz grade in her biology class, she has performed well otherwise and expects to receive the green color signals associated with positive course performance and strong likelihood of course success. However, when Alicia clicks on her alert, she becomes confused and dismayed. Despite doing well and receiving green signals for the majority of her classes, she has received a red signal for her biology class. With the signal comes a recommendation from the system to reach out to her faculty member or advisor for advice. Disheartened that one quiz grade would result in a red signal and confused about what yellow and red might mean, she thinks about what to do next: talk to her professor or drop the class?

Jon has been a professional advisor for more than 10 years. In that time, he has developed a number of systems to help him keep track of the more than 200 students that are on his caseload each academic year. Also in that time, the university has purchased a number of tools that it has promised will make intrusive advising of students easier. The latest tool purchased by the university is analytics based. The vendors in their promotional session promised that their tool will allow Jon to easily access student data, take notes on advising sessions, see trends across groups of students and courses, and provide more informed advising for students through data that can predict their likelihood of success in a given major. Although Jon likes the idea of understanding the trends in student course taking and success, he is concerned about protecting student privacy and is wary to put any personal notes related to his advising sessions into the new analytics tool, so he keeps a separate spreadsheet for note-keeping. He also values the time he spends interacting face to face with students and worries that will be lost through use of this tool. Most important, he worries about how predictive data might bias him or might have a negative impact on his students. Although the tool provides interesting information, it is not necessarily tailored to his approach to advising. Jon decides to rely on the homegrown tools he has developed over the past decade rather than using the new tool.

Sitting in a faculty senate meeting, Assistant Professor Erin Kelly has learned that her university has purchased a learning analytics tool to help with course retention and completion. She is intrigued about ways in which she could incorporate this tool into her teaching. According to university, the tool has the capability for faculty to reach out to students at risk of failing a course when there is still time to address their performance and progress. Through the learning analytics tool, Erin would be able to identify individual students at risk based on current and prior performance and on demographic data that have been linked to higher attrition rates, like college and high school GPA, socioeconomic background, work status (number of hours and on- versus off-campus employment), and status as a historically represented minority or first-generation student. Because Erin teaches a large survey course in biology, she is curious as to how this tool could help her better communicate with and better support her students. However, she is also concerned that having access to prior and predictive data about students could inadvertently bias her perspectives of those students. She is also uncomfortable with the underlying algorithm used to predict student success and concerned that using historical and demographic variables limits the influence of educational process and could potentially harm students' self-perceptions. Also, as a tenure-track faculty member, she is struggling to understand how she could incorporate this tool into her practice, given the demands on her time. Not sure what to do, Erin decides to learn more before committing to the new technology.

Introduction

The second chapter provided an overview of the organizational and technological factors that exist within the context of learning analytics implementation and adoption in higher education. In this chapter, we focus on the aspects of individual decision making that exist within that context for faculty, advisors, and students like Erin, Jon, and Alicia. Faculty, advisors, and students are increasingly interacting with learning analytics, whether or not they are aware of it. As stated in prior chapters, data from learning management system (LMS) (for example, Blackboard and Moodle) are being mined and incorporated into learning analytics algorithms that provide data visualizations and performance feedback related to teaching, advising, and course performance. LMS and learning analytics tools are examples of changing pedagogical innovations that have been deployed and leveraged as a way to improve institutional and individual decision making (Bichsel, 2012; Dahlstrom et al., 2014; Macfadyen & Dawson, 2012). However, these tools are useful to higher education only if individuals decide to adopt them. For faculty and advisors, like Jon and Erin, this decision making is often rooted in professional identity, beliefs, and behaviors. For students, like Alicia, although use of these tools is often required for course taking and course management, they still make active decisions about how to interpret and whether to act on the data provided through learning analytics visualizations. This chapter begins with a review of the literature related to the connection between faculty identity, beliefs, and behaviors and their decisions to use learning analytics tools. It concludes with an exploration of student use of learning analytics tools and their reactions to tool interventions.

Faculty and Advisor Decision Making

There has generally been uneven adoption of educational technology tools, including learning analytics, by faculty and advisors (Bichsel, 2012; Norris & Baer, 2013). In their survey of university faculty, Dahlstrom et al. (2014) found that less than half of surveyed faculty use LMS regularly and most faculty do not use these systems to their full capabilities. There is little empirical evidence as to why this uneven adoption exists and why some faculty and advisors choose not to use these tools. Current studies on learning analytics adoption primarily focus on students and their outcomes; although there are studies that have assessed faculty and advisor experiences related to use. Despite the paucity of literature specific to decisions by faculty and advisors to adopt learning analytics tools, the literature on faculty pedagogical change provides insight into the complexity around individual faculty decisions to incorporate innovations like learning analytics into their practice.

Specifically, faculty identity, beliefs, and behaviors affect decision making by creating potential barriers to adoption of new practices, including learning analytics (Bichsel, 2012; Dahlstrom et al., 2014; Norris & Baer, 2013). As stated in the second chapter for the Austin (2011) model, we argue that the literature on faculty decision making and change related to pedagogy can be extended to professional advising staff in higher education, because advising is acknowledged to be a teaching practice (Appleby, 2008; Crookston, 1994; Hagen & Jordan, 2008) and because advisors are often frontline users of technologies, like learning analytics tools.

Professional Identity

Faculty and advisor decision making is strongly tied to professional identity. Faculty and advisors have strong beliefs and socialized behavioral norms that can act as barriers to the incorporation of innovations, especially technological ones, into practice (Austin, 2011, 2003; Fairweather, 2002, 2008; Hora & Holden, 2013). These strongly held beliefs and behaviors are established and continued through disciplinary socialization (Amey, 1999; Austin, 2003, 2011; Fairweather, 2002, 2008; Locke, 1995; Tagg, 2012). Because professional identity is central to an individual's working role, aspects of that identity and how it is developed and cultivated over time can either promote or create barriers to adoption of new practices, including incorporation of technological innovations like learning analytics (Bichsel, 2012; Dahlstrom et al., 2014; Norris & Baer, 2013).

Professional identity is shaped through the socialization and acculturation that take place within their disciplines and within the academy at large. This process has an impact on whether faculty adopt or reject new approaches to teaching pedagogy, course design, and student advising (Austin, 2011; Brownell & Tanner, 2012; D'Avanzo, 2013; Fairweather, 2008; Sunal et al., 2001). Professional identity as shaped by socialization is one of the strongest barriers to individual change. Brownell and Tanner (2012) argue that the role of disciplinary training and professional identity supersedes other barriers to faculty change, including a lack of time and a lack of organizational incentives or rewards. Austin (2011) concurs, stating that socialization of doctoral students and early faculty created "values and norms" that are embedded in new faculty ways of being (p. 5). Tagg (2012) argues that there is a pattern of behavioral resistance, especially when expertise and "familiar ways of teaching" are questioned (p. 1), so change agents must be aware and account for issues of risk and loss and comfort in the status quo when the unknown can affect issues of endowment (especially tenure).

The influence of socialization as a barrier as it relates to pedagogical approach appears to be particularly significant in science, technology, engineering, and mathematics (STEM) related fields. These fields are most often resistant to changes in their pedagogical approach (Austin, 2011; D'Avanzo, 2013; Fairweather, 2008; Sunal et al., 2001). Sunal et al. (2001) note that the culture of science, "strong forces inhibiting change," and personal "beliefs and expectations about teaching and learning" both shape and inhibit change (p. 247). D'Avanzo (2013) found that science faculty may understand the need for change when confronted with the data, but that they lack an evidence-based path toward that change, consequently, "forward momentum will likely be limited, because we lack evidence-based, reliable models for actually realizing the desired 'change'" (p. 373). This resistance appears to be true even when faculty acknowledge reliable data related to shifting pedagogical needs and their associated benefits. Fairweather (2008) notes that "despite empirical evidence of effectiveness" of student learning outcomes related to pedagogical reforms, "the reforms died because no other faculty members were willing to invest in the time to teach the course in the new manner, in part because the time commitment was greater than traditional lectures" (p. 4). This is unsurprising as time constraints are not only a key factor in inhibiting pedagogical change among faculty but are also imbued in the academic environment (Austin, 2013; Fairweather, 2008).

Professional Beliefs

Faculty professional beliefs play a powerful and integral role in faculty decisions to adopt new technologies into practice (Hora & Holden, 2013; Kagan, 1992; Liu, 2011; Ottenbreit-Leftwich et al., 2010). Although the relationship between belief and behavior has been documented, beliefs vary by individual, they are composed of unconscious values and assumptions related to teaching, learning, and pedagogy (Kagan, 1992; Ottenbreit-Leftwich et al., 2010). For higher education faculty, these values and assumptions are shaped by the disciplinary socialization process (Austin, 2011). Faculty are more likely to incorporate innovations into their pedagogical practices when they possess an inherent appreciation of technology and when they can see the value of incorporating that technology (Ottenbreit-Leftwich et al., 2010).

These beliefs about technology have a strong hold over decision making, often superseding direct experiences, even when those experiences are positive (Ertmer, 2005; Ertmer et al., 2012; Hora & Holden, 2013; Liu, 2011). The influence beliefs have on behaviors is based on their existence as internal, or second-order, and external, or first-order, barriers (Ertmer et al., 2012). Second-order barriers related to technology adoption (for example, internal beliefs related to technology efficacy and value, teacher confidence, and student learning) have long been thought to be stronger inhibitors to behavior change than external or first-order barriers like "resources, training and support" (Ertmer et al, p. 423). Faculty must believe that an innovation or technology is useful, applicable, capable, and flexible to their needs and desires (Hora & Holden, 2013; Venkatesh & Bala, 2008). The strength of both second- and first-order barriers lies in their connection with an individual's belief system; because beliefs are the foundation upon which behavior, like decisions to integrate technology, develops. For faculty to decide to adopt a technology, they must not just experience its usefulness but first believe that it is relevant, useful, and tailored to their needs and interests (Hora & Holden, 2013; Meltzer & Manivannan, 2002; Venkatesh & Bala, 2008). Moreover, they need to see a congruence between their beliefs and the technology to change their behaviors (Ertmer, 2005; Ertmer et al., 2012; Hora & Holden, 2013; Liu, 2011; Ottenbreit-Leftwich et al., 2010).

Professional Behaviors

Faculty and advisor behaviors are affected by their disciplines and by socialization into their roles. Numerous studies have shown that disciplinary difference and socialization can affect decisions to adopt or reject new approaches to teaching, course design, and student advising (Austin, 2011; Brownell & Tanner, 2012; Fairweather, 2008). Socialization and professional identity are deeply embedded and can create strong barriers to change (Austin, 2011; Brownell & Tanner, 2012). Fairweather (2008) notes that even when shown proof of efficacy of student learning outcomes related to pedagogical reforms, faculty are unlikely to adopt those reforms, because learning and teaching in new ways require a greater time commitment than continuing to use traditional or habitual practices.

Although the literature is more focused on faculty, both faculty and advisors are affected by a lack of time coupled with a lack of rewards, incentives, and training. Incentives often propel faculty away from teaching and toward research (Amey, 1999; Austin, 2003, 2011; Fairweather, 2002, 2008; Locke, 1995; Tagg, 2012), which results in less time for learning and incorporating new technologies (Austin, 2011; Zellweger-Moser, 2007a, 2007b). Tagg (2012) argues that because a pattern of behavioral resistance exists, especially when expertise and "familiar ways of teaching" (p. 1) are questioned, change agents must be aware and account for issues of risk, loss, and comfort in the status quo when the unknown can affect issues of endowment (especially tenure). As a participant in one of the studies we conducted related to faculty decision making stated, her focus is on "publish, publish, publish." This need to focus on research limited the time to invest in learning new technologies (Klein et al., 2016b). For advisors, whose caseloads can exceed 200 students or more in a given semester, time is also a precious commodity. Further, our work has also found that although they are encouraged by supervisors, advisors, like faculty, receive no incentives to consistently incorporate new technologies, including learning analytics tools, into their practice (Klein et al., 2016b).

Beyond a lack of incentive is a lack of training to encourage decisions by faculty and advisors to use learning analytics tools. Institutions rarely provide individuals with the training and professional development opportunities necessary to encourage changes in pedagogical practice (Austin, 2011; Zellweger-Moser, 2007a, 2007b). Our work has also found that professional development and training that are tailored to roles and individual needs of faculty and advisors are also not commonly provided by higher education institutions, thus further limiting the chances that faculty and advisors will use these tools (Klein et al., 2016a, 2016b).

Professional identity, beliefs, and behaviors can create significant barriers to adoption of new technologies, primarily because change requires effort and "inertia, defense of the status quo, denial, and opposition and resistance to change" are often more natural places for faculty (and advisors) to reside (Jaffee, 1998, p. 22). However, there are ways that beliefs can be shifted to encourage a change in behaviors, which can ultimately have an impact on decisions to change and incorporate learning analytics tools. In our work, faculty and advisors consistently stated that they would be more likely to incorporate these tools if they were included in the design, development, and implementation process. Often, people we interviewed, advisors in particular, felt that learning analytics tools were developed in a bubble, without an understanding of the particularities of their roles or needs. If they were included in the process, they would be more likely to trust the tools. They argued that inclusion engendered trust, which engendered a greater likelihood that they would regularly use and incorporate learning tools into their work. Trust and inclusion are then key factors within higher education institutions that can be leveraged to encourage greater use of learning analytics by faculty and staff.

Impact of Identity, Beliefs, and Behaviors and Future Work

For learning analytics use in higher education, understanding how faculty choose to engage with these tools is key. The values that faculty and advisors bring to their careers influence their choices. For Jon, who values face-to-face interaction with his students and who had developed trusted tools that he believes allow him to effectively manage his workload, the idea of relying on learning analytics tools as a frontline means of advising does not comport with his professional ways of being. For Erin, who is committed to seeing her students succeed, the idea of a tool that could support them by alerting them to potential risks makes the idea of incorporating learning analytics tools intriguing; however, that is only if she understands how the tool works. Consequently, for learning analytics tools to be used, faculty and advisors must see a connection to their professional philosophies. Future work should try to better understand how these philosophies affect learning analytics adoption.

Student Decision Making

In the opening vignette, Alicia was grappling with deciding how to act after receiving an alert through her campus's learning analytics tool that indicated she was at risk for failing her course. Although the information provided to Alicia was meant to help her by prompting her to meet with her faculty member, she felt confused about how to act after receiving it. Student decision making (and decision making, generally) is notoriously complex. It is composed of aspects of self-efficacy, confidence, motivation, affect, and goals (Bandura, 1997; Chemers, Hu, & Garcia, 2001). Students experience many of the same issues as faculty and staff related to their decisions to use learning analytics tools. However, they are often affected differently as a result of using these tools. For faculty and advisors, the intent of learning analytics tools is to increase efficiency and effectiveness of advising and teaching by providing real-time feedback mechanisms and by allowing them to monitor student performance and progress and intervene with students at risk. For students, reception of their data and interventions through learning analytics tools can have a significant impact on their academic choices, self-perception, and subsequent course-related actions. This section of the chapter focuses on how students receive and make sense of their data and of the interventions that learning analytics tools provide. We provide an overview of learning analytics dashboards and components, followed by the impact of these tools on student decision making.

Learning Analytics Dashboards

Students access learning analytics tools via their dashboards. These learning dashboards are the interface components of learning analytics tools and the way in which students can interact with their data. Learning analytics dashboards can be used to measure, analyze, predict, and improve student engagement, retention, and completion rates and can provide course performance feedback and major and career recommendations (Arnold & Pistilli, 2012; Baker & Yacef, 2009; Ben-Naim et al., 2009; Bichsel, 2012; Dahlstrom et al., 2014; Macfadyen & Dawson, 2012; Mazza & Dimitrova, 2007; Norris & Baer, 2013; Peña-Ayala, 2014). These dashboards create an "interactive, historical, personalized, and analytical monitoring display that reflects students' learning patterns, status, performance, and interactions" (Park & Jo, 2015, p. 112). Ideally, the data communicated to students are offered in easily understandable visualizations that illuminate the "current and historical state of a learner or a course to enable flexible decision making" (Verbert et al., 2013).

Beyond providing real-time feedback to learners, learning analytics dashboards and the data underlying them have also been used to predict and communicate the likelihood of a student successfully passing courses or their aptitude in various majors (Arnold & Pistilli, 2012; Irvin & Longmire, 2016). Although not an exhaustive list, as of 2016, the following learner-specific dashboards had been developed for or were used in higher education institutions: Blackboard Learn, Civitas, Course Signals, Degree Compass, GLASS, LAPA, Moodle, Open Academics Analytics Initiative (OAAI), RioPACE, SNAPP, Student Activity Meter (SAM), Step Up!, Student Inspector, Student Success Collaborative (EAB), Tell Me More, and Narcissus.

Although learning analytics dashboards are being developed to increase student retention and completion rates, as was mentioned in the introduction of this monograph, students often act in opposition to the intended purposes of these tools by choosing to drop instead of completing courses (Jayaprakash et al., 2014). Like with faculty and advisors, student decision making related to learning analytics tools is equally complex and informed by a variety of factors. The unexpected reaction to learning analytics dashboard data by students may be caused in part by a misalignment in interpretation of the data, use of the dashboards, or a lack of trust in the data that are provided through dashboards (Duval, 2011; Jayaprakash et al., 2014; Park & Jo, 2015; Verbert et al., 2013, 2014).

Verbert et al. (2013) argue that student decision making is complex and that to work effectively, dashboards must provide data that "can be related to goals and progress toward these can be tracked, meaningful feedback loops can be created that can sustain desired behavior" (p. 1502). They propose a four-stage model related to learning analytics dashboard use as a way for learners to interpret these feedback loops in various stages that link cognition and action. Their model includes awareness (visualization of data), reflection (user assessment of data relevance), sensemaking (answering reflection questions and creating new insights), and impact (end goal—creating new meaning/creating behavioral change) (Verbert et al., 2013, pp. 1501–1502). Importantly, they note that the impact stage has yet to be effectively measured by current evaluation studies. Current tools are limited to a feedback loop among the first three stages (Verbert et al., 2013). The challenge in understanding the impact of these tools on students likely arises from the complex nature of student perceptions and behaviors related to learning analytics use.

Impact of Learning Analytics Dashboards on Student Actions

Studies have offered mixed results related to whether or not learning analytics improves learning outcomes, although a number of studies have cited student-perceived usefulness of these tool in reflecting on their coursework, tracking grades, and communicating with faculty and peers (Arnold & Pistilli, 2012; Kosma et al., 2005; Verbert et al., 2013, 2014). Of the evaluative studies related to student perceptions and use of learning analytics, Arnold and Pistilli (2012) offer one of the more comprehensive reports. Their Course Signals (CS) dashboard and underlying algorithm were developed at Purdue as a means of improving course retention. The use of the CS, in conjunction with instructor communication, was deemed helpful and motivating (74% said they were positively influenced) in changing their behavior. Of the 1,500 participants, most considered the learning analytics dashboards useful and minimized their sense of "being just a number." Only two negatively responded to communications from instructors. Others voiced concern about a lack of updating and real-time information related to their personal learning analytics dashboards.

As with Course Signals, Santos, Verbert, Govaerts, and Duval (2013) gathered student feedback on StepUp!, another learning analytics dashboard.

They found that student perception varied by background (demographics) and student type (class standing and courses taken) but that students valued opportunities for reflection and increased their collaboration levels as a result of dashboard use. Generally, students stated that the learning analytics dashboard allowed them to consider how they used their time, that communication was important, and that they liked being able to see how they worked with teammates. Concerns included that the dashboard did not increase their motivation, did not allow them to compare themselves to others, and did not help elucidate course problems. Despite issues with StepUp! students rated the tool between acceptable and good. Researchers found that social interaction increased collaboration levels in the course.

Despite the potential of learning analytics dashboards like CS and StepUp!, the intent of these tools often does not align with subsequent student action. As discussed previously, Jayaprakash et al. (2014) provide an overview of the OAAI at Marist College and subsequent student reactions to their learning analytics dashboard. More than 1,700 students participated in the OAAI and 451 were deemed at risk. There was little to no significant difference between control and experimental groups across the measures used in the study. Surprisingly, students in the intervention groups withdrew at higher levels than the control groups, which is in direct opposition to the intended purpose of the tool's developers. It is unclear why students chose to withdraw. However, decisions to use data provided by dashboards and to act on their associated interventions may be rooted in student trust and understanding of the data they receive.

Duval (2011) found that learning analytics dashboards that provide a higher level of "attention trust" were deemed more useful and trustworthy by users. In this case, trust includes student consideration of property and data ownership, mobility of data, and transparency, like being able to compare their data to other students. Understanding the information that they are receiving also plays a role in student use of tools. Park and Jo (2015) created the LAPA learning analytics dashboard. As a part of development, they elicited student feedback on useful aspects of the LAPA. They found that, although students used LAPA at low levels, they were able to understand the data provided via the dashboard. Further, they found that overall satisfaction of the dashboard was a covariant with degree of understanding and associated behavioral changes in use of the tool. Park and Jo also found that, although dashboards display diverse data in both simple and complex ways, few learning analytics tools use dashboard design principles to display the data. The existence of difficult to understand data visualizations can affect student decisions and behaviors related to use of these tools.

Sensemaking and Trust

There are relatively few studies related to student interpretation of data visualization in dashboards. Most of the literature is descriptive of the various types of visualizations different tools use. Park & Jo (2015) in their analysis of learning analytics dashboards noted that a majority of tools used bar graphs, pie charts, sociograms, signal lights, and what-if analysis (win–lose) to display login trends, performance results, content usage, at-risk prediction, message analysis, and social networks. Demmans Epp & Bull (2015) do go beyond description to provide recommendations for data visualization that will minimize uncertainty and boost impact and action through use of visualization using visual variables (motion, position, arrangement, and so on), interpretability of visualized data, and learner modeling (ensuring user groups understand how to interpret data). Finally, Charleer, Klerkx, Odriozola, Luis, and Duval (2013) investigated the use of trace data and badging as a means to create a feedback loop of awareness, reflection, sensemaking, and impact—using Verbert et al.'s (2013) model. They used both a Naviboard (navigable dashboard) and a haptic (touch-sensitive) model Navitouch, both driven by a badging model. Although impact was not significant, the haptic model was more popular and perceived as more useful by users.

In our work (Klein et al., 2017), we have sought to increase understanding of the impact of learning analytics dashboards on sensemaking and subsequent action, beyond their reaction to visualized data. Our findings have affirmed prior literature by showing the multiple ways in which learning analytics data and visualizations affect students' perceptions and actions but also underscore some of the tension points that exist during the sensemaking process. Students want tools that could be both personalized and tailored to their needs but also that allow them to remain somewhat anonymous. They want to receive data but preferred delivery of data on a timeline and in a manner that they can control. Most important, students privilege their own assessment of current and performance over the predictive assessment of learning analytics algorithms.

Another unique aspect of our findings is the understanding that the tension points students experience are rooted in issues of trust. Duval (2011) argues that dashboard data must provide attention trust related to accuracy, transparency, and understanding. Further, Demmans Epp and Bull (2015) and Park and Jo (2015) have also argued that clear and understandable visualizations can increase student use of learning analytics dashboards. Certainly, trust in the data is important but so is the context from which that trust can be established.

Students are willing to consider and, further, trust data when they were contextualized for them. Colored signals or progress bars alone were unlikely to be understood or trusted by students, whereas context-rich data allowed students to trust what they were seeing. This trust provides a foundation from which students do not reject outright assessments on their current or future performance, but rather they can reflect on their performance, make sense of the data they are receiving, and potentially change future actions and behaviors. Student trust in data extends beyond the data points and their visualizations to an understanding of who is sending the data. An important finding is that students are more likely to trust academic data sent by a faculty member or advisor with whom they have a relationship. Nonacademic data (related to a student's integration on campus), data sent via an automated system, or communications sent from an unknown or untrusted faculty member or advisor were much less likely to be trusted.

For students like Alicia, having data that are provided to them via dashboards can be useful and can lead to improved outcomes, like meeting with faculty to discuss their performance and strategies for improvement or by increasing their study time, time on task, or class attendance. However, students are more likely to respond positively to dashboard data if those data are contextualized to their specific circumstances, if they are sent by a trusted faculty member, and if they are accompanied by a suggested course of action and resources for support.

Conclusion and Future Work

The second and third chapters have outlined the complexities of learning analytics implementation and adoption in higher education. From organizational to technological to individual factors, learning analytics face a variety of forces that can either promote or constrain its use by faculty, advisors, and students. Organizationally, the siloed structures of higher education institutions make implementation of change of any kind a challenge. However, those structures can be overcome if institutions have the capacity and are ready, via leadership, user buy-in and participation, financial, technical and personnel resources, and technological infrastructure, to implement learning analytics on their campuses. Technological issues are important to address prior to implementation. Otherwise, issues of integration, alignment, and user trust can derail efforts to improve learning analytics adoption rates. Learning analytics tools must be reliable and relevant for users to see the value in incorporating them into their practices. Including users in the development and acquisition process is a foundational way to improve technological aspects of adoption. Finally, decision making to use these tools is founded upon issues of identity, beliefs, and behaviors that can affect levels of trust in learning analytics tools. More needs to be done to understand how faculty, advisors, and students interpret learning analytics data, their reasons for adopting or rejecting these tools, and how these tools can be tailored to their specific needs.

Student, faculty, and advisor decision making related to learning analytics tools is an area ripe for future work. It is important to understand the impact of these tools on student decision making and the subsequent impact that decision making can have on their academic careers. Understanding how learning analytics dashboard data are consumed and interpreted by students like Alicia can help to create better tools that can better guide students in their decision making. As stated previously, for faculty and advisors like Jon and Erin, understanding how their professional philosophies affect their sensemaking related to learning analytics is equally important in creating tools that will be useful and supportive of their goals. Additional suggestions for future work in this area are explored in the fifth chapter.

Ethical and Privacy Concepts and Considerations

Jamal is a freshman at a large, research-intensive, public university in the United States. When he arrives on campus, orientation activities are in full swing. Jamal is given a password that gives him access to his campus email and learning management system. He also receives an ID card that he can use to gain access to his residence hall, to check in to campus offices and events, to borrow books from library, or to purchase items in the campus bookstore. Jamal is also led into a room where he is told to look into a viewfinder to have his iris scanned. The orientation employee tells Jamal that this will give him access to the dining halls on campus without an ID, which will protect his meal account if his ID is lost. It also saves the institution money (both on meals and the cost of ID scanners). Jamal asks if this is something he has to do. He is told that the scanning is mandatory—to have access to the meal plans in the student union dining halls, you must use the scanner. Jamal lives on campus so he has to buy his meals through the meal plan system. Feeling like he has no choice in the matter and wondering, really, what harm it can do, Jamal looks into the viewfinder.

Anna is an experienced professional advisor at Jamal's university, and she is busy. Anna's student workload includes more than 400 students. Anna's institution has just purchased a new learning

analytics advising tool that incorporates student admission, regis-
tration, academic, and extracurricular data as a means to help with
her workload. Anna's supervisor tells her that use of this new tool
will dramatically improve her ability to advise her students because
the tool allows her to manage her caseload and share information
with her colleagues across campus departments. Her supervisor also
indicates that use of this tool is expected. After a brief website train-
ing provided via the tool's vendor, Anna logs on to use the tool. As
promised, the tool provides detailed data on students—including
data on everything from course performance to advising history to
participation in on-campus activities to family demographics. It
also allows her to group students by major and cocurricular in-
terests. However, Anna quickly becomes concerned that if she uses
this tool's notetaking component to share information with her col-
leagues, she will be violating the Family Educational Rights and
Privacy Act. Not wanting to violate FERPA, Anna decides to use
the tool to gain access to student data but defers to her homegrown
notetaking system, preferring to keep all notes on student advising
meetings off of this new system.

Assistant Professor Erica Paredes is in her third year of teaching a
spring semester intro to biology course for freshmen. This year, she
has been invited to participate in a test pilot of a new predictive an-
alytics tool. The tool allows her to view student course performance
data (both her course, concurrent courses, and courses taken in the
previous semester) and uses an algorithm, based on student demo-
graphics, high school GPA, residential status, prior course data, and
other factors to predict student course performance. Although Erica
is intrigued by this new tool, she is wary of the data it provides.
She wonders whether seeing student data from outside of her course
might bias her in any way. As a research faculty member, although
she values data, she also chafes at the idea of having a tool prescribe
an outcome for a student and questions the use of demographic
data used in the tool's algorithm. However, her class is large and

demanding, and the tool's vendors promise that the tool can help
her identify and help struggling students sooner. Erica decides to use
the tool and participates in the test pilot.

Introduction

These vignettes illustrate some of the ethical and privacy-related challenges
that are associated with learning analytics in higher education. Although
Jamal's experience may sound like the ominous introduction to a dystopian
science fiction film, student data—even biometric data like iris scans—are
currently being collected by higher education institutions. The goals of data
collection in higher education address a variety of purposes, ranging from improving student retention and completion outcomes to monitoring cocurricular activity participation for assessment purposes to minimizing fraudulent
use of campus resources. With the advent of data mining and learning analytics technology, these data can be collected in vast amounts from numerous sources that can "open up new and unanticipated uses of information"
(Steiner, Kickmeier-Rust, & Albert, 2016, p. 68).

The use of learning analytics for improved institutional performance and
student retention and completion has become an increasingly important focus of higher education institutions (Slade & Prinsloo, 2013; Steiner et al.,
2016). Learning analytics has so much purported potential and has become
so important that Slade and Prinsloo (2013) argue that higher education institutions cannot afford not to begin using educational big data. Although
learning analytics can offer new insights into higher education institutions,
faculty, students, and staff, boundaries around use of these data are often ill
defined and questions about ethical use of the data and protection of student
privacy abound (Pardo & Siemens, 2014; Slade & Prinsloo, 2013; Steiner
et al., 2016).

From issues of security and harm to concerns about privacy violations
or biased decision making, ethics, and privacy are an important, yet emergent and often ill-defined component of learning analytics. Learning analytics
tools and the data and algorithms upon which they rely are rapidly evolving.
As with other technological advances, although learning analytics developers

and researchers acknowledge the importance of considering ethics and privacy during the development and implementation of learning analytics tools, associated policies, procedures, and best practices related to ethics and privacy often lag behind tool development (Prinsloo & Slade, 2015; Willis, 2014; Willis & Pistilli, 2014).

As a result of this lag, "definitions, as well as our legal and regulatory frameworks often struggle to keep up with the technological developments and changing societal norms" (Prinsloo & Slade, 2015). Consequently, relatively few frameworks exist that have integrated issues related to learning analytics ethics and privacy (Prinsloo & Slade, 2015; Slade & Prinsloo, 2013). Most of the literature reviewed for this text noted the relative absence of research publications focused on ethics and privacy (Drachsler et al., 2015; Ferguson, Hoel, Scheffel, & Drachsler, 2016; Prinsloo & Slade, 2015; Rubel & Jones, 2016; Sclater, 2016; Steiner et al., 2016; Swenson, 2014). Swenson's (2014) review of abstracts submitted to the Learning Analytics Knowledge (LAK) conference in 2014 found that less than 3% dealt with learning analytics privacy policies. In a similar review of the conference's presentations, Drachsler et al. (2015) found that only a small fraction of papers referred to privacy and of those 12 only 3 actively addressed issues of privacy related to privacy protection. The rest referred to privacy as a barrier or restriction to learning analytics development (Drachsler et al., 2015).

The reference to ethics and privacy by learning analytics scholars and developers as "constraints," "barriers," and "impediments" is not uncommon and has been a traditional way of viewing these concepts (Ferguson et al., 2016; Gašević, Dawson, & Jovanović, 2016; Khalil & Ebner, 2014; Sclater, 2016). Researchers referring to ethics and privacy in this way often view these aspects of learning analytics as impeding technological advancement and limiting the power of the tool and its impact on student outcomes (Ferguson et al., 2016; Gašević et al., 2016). Drachsler et al. (2015) argue that for learning analytics to benefit organizations, privacy must be accounted for and overcome.

Situating ethics and privacy as problems to be fixed rather than opportunities to refine and improve learning analytics tools is ultimately problematic as individual use of these tools is dependent upon the accuracy, trustworthiness, and transparency of the data provided therein (Sclater, 2016; Slade & Prinsloo, 2013; Steiner et al., 2016). Gašević et al. (2016) recently addressed the negative slant given to ethics and privacy by "encouraging the [learning analytics] community to see ethics and privacy as enablers rather than barriers" (p. 2) to learning analytics adoption, stating learning analytics use will become broadly adopted only when concerns related to ethics and privacy are addressed.

How ethics and privacy are defined and conceptualized affect how they are incorporated and addressed in learning analytics and, ultimately, how users experience these tools. This chapter explores the various conceptions of ethics and privacy in learning analytics and their associated challenges and opportunities. Specifically, the chapter provides an overview and analysis of current literature and issues related to learning analytics ethics and privacy, including definitions; current contexts, considerations, policies, and best practices; proposed frameworks for understanding and addressing ethics and privacy; and future work to be done.

Ethics and Privacy: Definitions, Conceptions, and Influences

To understand the effects of learning analytics on ethics and privacy, it is important to first define these terms both as they stand on their own and in their relationship to educational big data. There are numerous nuanced definitions related to ethics and privacy and multiple perspectives on how these concepts are related. Importantly, traditional conceptions of agency and privacy are often not adequate to address the rapidly evolving data mining and analytics fields, which require specific considerations related to transparency, control, and security of data (Pardo & Siemens, 2014; Prinsloo & Slade, 2015; Sclater, 2016; Steiner et al., 2016). What follows is a review of the various definitions of and relationships between ethics and privacy, as explained by learning analytics scholars, and a consideration of the strengths and challenges of current conceptions related to these terms as they relate to learning analytics, specifically, and within the specific context of higher education.

Evolving Definitions and Concepts

In their 2016 article that offers a checklist for privacy and ethics issues in learning analytics, Drachsler and Geller also provide a brief evolution of the thinking around privacy. As they note, early ideas of privacy revolved around the "right to be let alone" (Warren & Brandie, 1890, cited in Drachsler & Greller, 2016, p. 3), but ethics related to privacy is in a consistent state of evolution, as individuals negotiate trade-offs between the right for privacy and a desire for disclosure and social norms. Drachsler and Greller also provide useful definitions for ethics and privacy and lay out the relationship between these concepts. They argue that ethics "is the philosophy of morality that involves systematizing, defending, and recommending concepts of right and wrong conduct" and "privacy is a living concept made out of continuous personal boundary negotiations with the surrounding ethical environment" (pp. 2–3). Therefore, ethics are a fluctuating "moral code of norms and conventions that exist in society externally to a person, whereas privacy is an intrinsic part of a person's identity and integrity" (Drachsler & Geller, pp. 2–3).

These definitions of ethics and privacy are based on both historical understandings of these concepts and an awareness of the influence of new technologies, which Westin (1968) argued introduces new and shifting issues of power between the individual, society, and technology (Drachsler & Greller, 2016). There are specific ethical and privacy-related concerns within an increasingly technological and data-rich environment. Within this environment, conceptions related to ethical considerations of privacy have moved beyond notions of control of individual information toward a theoretical model that is based on context, concept, justification, and management of information (Heath, 2014).

Among the most cited modern privacy theories espoused by learning analytics scholars is contextual integrity. Contextual integrity, as argued by Nissenbaum (2004), is the idea that although control and access of information exists in considering privacy, privacy in the modern era is associated with and regulated by the flow of information based on norms that are context-relative. These norms include context, actors, attributes, and transmission principles and they affect the flow of information from information senders to information receivers to information subjects (Nissenbaum, 2004). Barth, Datta, Mitchell, and Nissenbaum (2006) argue that using contextual integrity as an ethical framework for considering how information moves from one party to another can "provide guidance on how to respond to conflicts between values and interests and to provide a systematic setting for understanding privacy" (p. 1).

Although contextual integrity is useful in understanding how information moves from one agent to another, it does not speak specifically to the potential tensions that might arise from that flow of information. Because learning analytics data use large data sets that are often repurposed from prior data collected for specific reasons, the contextuality of collected data is affected, violating data integrity (Drachsler & Greller, 2016). This is a problem for learning analytics as it relates to privacy under a contextual integrity framework, because learning analytics is dependent upon data that are not temporally or contextually bound. Consequently, it requires an understanding of the privacy-related tensions that emerge when data are repurposed and used in learning analytics, especially in predictive analysis. Pardo and Siemens (2014) argue that tension exists "between the private and public information from the self to others" and that tension related to privacy is heightened when data from the past are used to predict future actions (Palen & Dourish, 2003, p. 440). The unique and increasingly ubiquitous nature of learning analytics data requires a shift in thinking the ethical policies and practices related to individual privacy.

As a result of the emergent nature of the learning analytics field, there has been an evolution of thought related to ethics and privacy and to their domains of influence. Pardo and Siemens (2014) provide a definition for privacy that is based on its relationship to learning analytics, arguing that "privacy is defined as the regulation of how personal digital information is being observed by the self or distributed to other observers" (p. 438). They further argue that ethics is the "systemization of correct and incorrect behavior in virtual spaces according to all stakeholders (p. 439). The definitions provided by Pardo and Siemens are useful in that they provide utilitarian understanding of these concepts but also speak to issues of power, surveillance, feedback, and action that are inherent in learning analytics systems.

This nuanced understanding is important, as definitions and modeling alone are not enough to understand the issues related to privacy and ethics. The inherent tensions within these conceptions need to be explored and interrogated, as Willis (2014) argues that discussions of learning analytics and ethics are underdeveloped (p. 1). The problem, he argues, lies in the binary, right versus wrong utilitarianism that seeks to minimize harm by doing the "most good for the most people" (Willis, 2014, p. 2), but understanding what constitutes "good" is often impossible, given the unique contexts in which learning analytics exists. To address the use of utilitarianism as a sole means for determining ethical use of learning analytics, Willis proposes the use of framework situated in moral utopianism, ambiguity, and nihilism that can address some of the context-based tensions that emerge in learning analytics systems.

Through the use of this moral framework, Willis (2014) argues that analytics developers and institutional administrators should ask "probing questions, assessments of possible outcomes and active disagreement about future developments" (p. 4). These questions encourage the questioning of biases and assumptions and are based on ideas of how a system might be developed and operated within a perfect world, creating no negative impact and improving outcomes for all (utopianism); within an uncertain world, wherein outcomes are unclear or unintentional (ambiguity); and within a meaningless world with valueless outcomes and impacts (nihilism) (Willis). Although highly theoretical in nature, the benefit of Willis' ethical framework is that it allows everyone involved in the development and implementation of learning analytics to consider ethical questions, assumptions, and impacts of this technology.

Despite numerous and evolving definitions and conceptions of ethics and privacy, these terms are often unclear and ill defined (Ferguson et al., 2016; Slade and Prinsloo, 2013). Given the complexities of various contexts and learning analytics, the inherent tensions that exist within those contexts and within learning analytics, and the nuanced nature of ethics and privacy concepts themselves, this is not a surprise. However, with each new conception comes a better understanding of the various components and influences that shape our ideas of societal ethics and individual privacy as they relate to learning analytics.

Ethics and Privacy Within the Higher Education Context

Further complicating definitions of ethics and privacy as they relate to learning analytics is the complex environment of higher education institutions. One of the missions of colleges and universities is to provide for the education and development of its students. Within this mission, the relationship between the institution and the student has evolved. Historically, higher education officials in the United States acted in loco parentis for students at their institutions, which allowed colleges and universities to act in lieu of parental involvement in internal affairs (Lake, 1999). This approach to the relationship between the institution and the individual student gave colleges and universities a monopoly of power and broad rights in decision making related to student academic, cocurricular, and personal affairs and acted as an insulating and protective mechanism for the institution and employees (Lake).

In the United States, with the advent of the GI Bill, the civil rights movement, reduced funding and increased corporatization, in loco parentis was not adequately addressing the shifting demographics, dynamics, and needs of higher education (Lake, 1999). This shift spurred institutions to move toward conceptualizing their relationship with students as one that requires a duty of care for the individual student's or the collective student body's well-being as a means to mitigate risk or harm (Lake, 1999; Willis, 2014). As a result, institutions "have a fiduciary duty and need to demonstrate care for the well-being and positive development of students, leading them to success in their studies" (Drachsler & Greller, 2016, p. 5). Moreover, institutions, once they have knowledge that can affect a student's well-being, have an obligation to act (Kay, Korn, & Oppenheim, 2012). However, establishing a duty of care also releases the institution from total power and control over from students, requiring that they act in good faith to care for the students at their institutions, but those students must also "take responsibility for their own choices and the inherent risks of the activities they choose" (Lake, 1999, p. 21). It is within this unique context that learning analytics conceptions of ethics and privacy are currently being considered, defined, and redefined, both in the United States and abroad.

For many in the field of learning analytics conceptualizing ethics and privacy as part of a duty to act is a relatively new way of thinking about these aspects of big data. Pardo and Siemens (2014) argue that reconceptualization of privacy and the ethical framework within which privacy is considered within the context of learning analytics is important as traditional conceptions "are no longer adequate to understand privacy" (p. 439). This is often because scholars and scientists in the learning analytics field have historically viewed ethical and privacy concerns as a "restriction on action rather than a call to action" (Ferguson et al., 2016, p. 8). However, as Ferguson et al. (2016) argue, when analytics are considered from a "duty to act" perspective, they can help promote the development of better analytics and associated tools and outcomes.

Institutional, Individual, and Data Considerations

Ethics and privacy considerations exist at multiple levels and are foundational to the use of learning analytics in higher education. From institutions and their roles in establishing policies and practices that protect its members and their data, to individuals and their rights, agency, and data ownership, to data and their security and validity, these considerations are integral to the creation, development, and implementation of learning analytics tools. As these tools increasingly being developed and used in higher education institutions, it is important to understand the interplay between existing contexts and potential ethics and privacy issues.

Institutional Contexts

Developers of learning analytics tools certainly should be actively approaching their work from an ethical standpoint and faculty, staff, and student users have the right to be actively involved in decisions that affect their privacy. However, perhaps the most important actors within the learning analytics field (arguably, the one with the most power and potential impact) are higher education institutions. Colleges and universities are not just the purchasers of learning analytics tools but are also its purveyors. Higher education institutions implement initiatives in which large amounts of data are collected and are the creators of the policies and practices that protect the data. Therefore, it is important to understand how institutions ethically approach use of learning analytics while maintaining users' privacy.

Slade and Prinsloo in their various works have provided the most comprehensive consideration of ethical and privacy considerations related to learning analytics in higher education (Prinsloo & Slade, 2013; Slade & Prinsloo, 2013, 2015). They note that there are numerous ethical issues that higher education institutions should consider, including the "location and interpretation of data, informed consent, privacy and de-identification of data; and management and classification and storage of data" (Prinsloo & Slade, 2013, p. 1). Among the issues they address are the influence of power, surveillance, and potential for harm in learning management systems and other learning analytics systems in use in higher education. They note that for higher education, the providers of learning analytics tools, "the power to harvest, analyse and exploit data lies completely with the providers" (Prinsloo & Slade, 2015, p. 6).

Given this power, learning analytics vendors and higher education institutions have a responsibility to address issues of potential harm. This is especially important to remember when working with dynamic and powerful learning analytics systems that include the potential for surveillance. Given their data-gathering potential, learning analytics could have the potential to keep users under constant surveillance and "[could] reveal things about them to others that they are not aware of themselves" (Ferguson et al., 2016, p. 11). However, there are also advantages to surveillance and Prinsloo and Slade (2015) argue that surveillance is a "necessary and crucial tool within the context of the social contract and duty of care" (p. 6).

But for learning analytics and a duty of care to work, everyone within the institution, administrators and students alike must agree that learning analytics, like other pedagogical tools and approaches, serve to improve student outcomes (Ferguson et al., 2016, pp. 11–12). The concerns related to privacy violations or the development of undue bias, like those that advisors like Anna and faculty like Erica encounter, must be addressed. This requires that higher education institutions work to "ensure transparency, security and reasonable care" of student privacy and data as a means to minimize harm (Drachsler & Greller, 2016; Prinsloo & Slade, 2015, p. 6).

How institutions address issues of power, surveillance, potential harm, privacy protection, and other ethical considerations are unique to the various institutions and are affected by an epistemological "understanding of the scope, role, and boundaries of learning analytics and a set of moral beliefs founded on the respective regulatory and legal, cultural, geopolitical, and socio-economic contexts" (Prinsloo & Slade, 2013, p. 2). For institutions and the individuals involved in learning analytics use, having an epistemological understanding is important as it can help ground use of learning analytics data within an ethical framework that aligns with the unique contexts, needs, and intentions of the data. This grounding allows for better interrogation of ethical considerations within these unique contexts.

Willis, Campbell, and Pistilli (2013) argue that use of learning analytics in higher education, especially around student retention, success, and completion, result in specific and practical ethical questions related to obligations to act, including what to do and what actions or answers are correct once knowledge is known about a specific student. To help answer these questions, they offer use of the Potter Box. The Potter Box is an ethical model used in business that allows for interrogation of assumptions around decision making (Willis et al.). Use of the Potter Box in higher education learning analytics is helpful in that it provides a foundational framework through the establishment of definitions, values, principles, and loyalties that address issues of ethical context, individual privacy and agency, and potential bias of learning analytics data within the unique context of an institution (Willis et al.).

Individual Contexts

Every time students log on to their learning management system or swipe their student identification into the library or residence hall, a data point is collected. Users give these data to their institutions either because they are not informed of the terms of using various data platforms or are resigned to those terms and because use of the LMS, library, or residence hall doors requires participation in the learning analytics system (Pardo & Siemens, 2014; Prinsloo & Slade, 2015). Consequently, students are engaged in constant negotiation, conscious or otherwise, between maintaining privacy and having access to important systems. Ideally, this negotiation would be an informed one, wherein students and other learning analytics users in higher education would be aware of what was being collected about them, could provide prior consent for that collection, and could trust the use of that collection. However, students, like Jamal in the introductory vignette, are often not informed as to how their data will be collected, analyzed, and used, and rarely are they given the opportunity to provide informed consent. Creating a process by which students can give informed consent and understand how their data are being used is especially important now, as vast amounts of personal information are being gathered, collected, and shared.

Consent and Agency

Consent allows for individuals to self-manage their privacy in relation to data that have been collected about them. Consent, or privacy self-management, is an important concept related to learning analytics ethics and privacy. Prinsloo and Slade (2015) argue that "consent is an undertheorized concept that is crucial for privacy" (p. 2), and Steiner et al. (2016) contend that "consent needs to be recognized as a basic ethical principle and procedure" (p. 81). However, for consent to be relevant, individuals must understand what they are consenting to, including the types of data collected and the potential outcomes of providing access to that data (Prinsloo & Slade, 2015). Yet, often individuals are not aware of what data are being collected or how the data are being used (Ferguson et al., 2016).

Much of this lack of understanding and awareness is because individuals are not aware of and may not be able to comprehend the amount of data collected by analytics tools and the potential impacts of that use (Prinsloo & Slade, 2015, p. 3). Moreover, learning analytics vendors and higher education institutions do not make individual users aware of types of data that are being collected and the ethical and privacy boundaries associated with that collection (Drachsler & Greller, 2016). Establishment of consent in learning analytics has not been an historical prerequisite. Prinsloo and Slade (2015) note that there is "little or no published research or theorizing in the context of higher education whether students should have the option to opt-out of having their learning data harvested, analysed and used" despite the fact that this could increase transparency and trust (p. 2).

Consideration of consent as optional is beginning to change, as scholars see the value of collaborating with students to improve analytics use. Slade and Prinsloo (2014) argue that institutions must collaborate with students to create an environment of informed consent in which students freely provide data that will ultimately support their learning and growth. By treating students as collaborators in learning analytics, they contend that students will not only consent to data collection but will "voluntarily collaborate in providing data and access to data to allows learning analytics to serve *their* learning and development, and not just the efficiency of institutional profiling and interventions" (Slade & Prinsloo, 2014, p.13). There is no good reason, as Steiner et al. (2016) argue that waivers of consent should exist because consent should always be required. The decision to provide consent should be given freely by users who are informed of the parameters of data collection, analysis, and use and analytics vendors and higher education institutions should ensure that users have adequate information from which to make that choice. However, for collaboration and consent of this nature to work users must trust both their institutions and the learning analytics tools they are being asked to use (Ferguson et al., 2016).

Trust and Bias

Despite the potential for ethical and privacy violations in learning analytics work, there are relatively few studies that query users for their perceptions related to these tools. However, there are indications that data subjects are concerned about privacy within the context of increased data mining, surveillance, and analytics (Prinsloo & Slade, 2015). In their survey of K–16 education administrators, Drachsler and Greller (2012) found that 65.8% of their 123 respondents "believe[d] that learning analytics will affect privacy and personal affairs" and 60.1% were concerned about data ownership and intellectual property (p. 5). In addition, many administrators simply were unsure of what impact learning analytics could have on their institutions and students, indicating a need for further education in this area (Drachsler & Geller, 2012).

In our two recent studies related to use of learning analytics, we conducted focus groups with faculty, advisors, and students. Students expressed a wariness over the types of information collected and how that information was shared but also indicated a general inevitability that their data would be used, beyond their control, by their institution (Klein et al., 2017). Moreover, they were unlikely to trust or believe data that did not conform to their own conceptions about themselves and their potential (Klein et al., 2017). Like the Erica and Anna in the opening vignettes, participants in our study were concerned about the potential bias that might emerge from having additional and predictive data from learning analytics data or that they might violate FERPA laws (Klein et al., in press). Although they generally wanted to know more about their students, this desire was balanced by a concern that knowledge might inadvertently predispose them to predetermining student outcomes. The concerns expressed by participants in both studies illuminate the inherent complexities of learning analytics data.

Data Considerations

Data do not exist in a vacuum; they are affected by the environment from which they are culled. Within learning analytics, issues of bias, transparency, security, and access have emerged as key factors related to ethical development and privacy protection.

Algorithmic Bias

Learning analytics are based on algorithms. An algorithm is a "finite sequence of well-defined instructions that describe in sufficiently great detail how to solve a problem" (Kraemer, Overveld, & Peterson, 2011, p. 251). With the dawn of data mining, the algorithms that drive learning analytics have become ubiquitous, and although they can provide new insights into institutional and student performance, they are also subject to bias. Algorithmic bias occurs when the algorithms, based on human and technological errors (via input factors or correlations in the data), create discriminatory outcomes (Bozdag, 2013; Diakopoulos, 2015; Hajian, Bonchi, & Castillo, 2016).

Algorithmic bias can occur "even when there is no discrimination intention in the developer of the algorithm" and, even when accounted for, "well trained machine learning algorithms may still discriminate" (Hajian et al., 2016, p. 1). This discrimination can occur because algorithms are based on "implicit or explicit value judgements" that force choices (Kraemer et al., 2011, p. 252). The problem with algorithmic bias is not just the potential for discrimination but the scale at which it can affect learning analytics users. Because algorithms often lack transparency, algorithmic opacity clouds an understanding of what learning analytics data are founded upon. As Diakopoulos (2015) argues, the problem with opacity is that makes it difficult to understand the scale and complexity of algorithms, which can lead "to a lack of clarity for the public in terms of how they exercise their power and influence" (p. 398). Because algorithmic bias and opacity can affect user interpretation of data, despite its purported predictive power, algorithms can also be wrong (Gillespie, 2012). The danger of this potential error is that it can "continue to perpetuate 'old prejudices'" (Rubel & Jones, 2016, p. 147; Tene & Polonetsky, 2013, p. 254). For learning analytics to be seen as valid and trustworthy, the value-laden nature of algorithms must be addressed.

Transparency and Trust

For learning analytics users to use and act on the information and interventions they receive, those data must be transparent and trustworthy. Pardo and Siemens (2014) argue that transparency should be addressed in all aspects of learning analytics and that trust is of paramount importance. Because the purpose of learning analytics is to spur individuals to action by offering data and performance feedback, issues of transparency and trust are tied to ethics and privacy. Learning analytics data need to be "representative, relevant, accurate and up-to-date" (Steiner et al., 2016, p. 84) because learning analytics users are making active decisions based on that data.

Transparency of both data and their use is important factor in learning analytics. Transparency goes beyond consent to include detailed information on who is collecting data, data use, data recipients, types of data collected, collection method, consequences of refusal, and measures taken to ensure high-quality data and security (Steiner et al., 2016). Transparency also deals with data accuracy and reliability. When using big data, the original purpose of the data, such as to track student course schedules, can be lost and the data used for other purposes, such as predicting student course grades.

Assumptions about the original intent may lead to false or questionable decisions and conclusions drawn as the data become decontextualized (Prinsloo & Slade, 2015, p. 4).

By providing open details, both transparency (including data reliability) and trust increase. Indeed, trust in systems is often dependent upon transparency. Beattie, Woodley, and Souter (2014) argue that "to earn the trust and encourage the engagement of students, learner data systems need to be open, rather than based on proprietary technologies, transparent, personalized, networked, transportable, adaptive and interactive" (p. 422). However, as Siemens (2012) notes many learning analytics tools are not open to researchers with open and accessible data (p. 2). Rubel and Jones (2016) concur, stating that although the goal of analytics are to provide a clearer, data-supported future, "the data they subsume and the resulting analytic products that influence the lives of individuals are black boxed" (Rubel & Jones, 2016, p. 147). The proprietary nature of learning analytics innovations unfortunately limits transparency of data, which in turn can affect trust.

Security, Access, and Ownership

In addition to transparency and trust, there are practical considerations related to ethical use of data and privacy protection. Among them are providing for data security and establishing rules for data access and ownership. Steiner et al. (2016) argue that it is important that structures be put in place to ensure the protection of user data against potential "unauthorized access, loss, destruction, or misuse" (p. 85). Among the structures necessary to protect users are those that indicate when data are at risk or are incorrect, those that require authentication and verification of identity for access, and those that can adequately manage files (Steiner et al., 2016). This is especially important given the vast amounts of data that are being collected and the implications associated with protecting the data.

In addition to security and access, data ownership is an important, but complex, component of ethics and privacy (Drachsler & Greller, 2016). As discussed previously, individuals should have full access to their data and be collaborative in the data collection process. Moreover, they should have the right to consent to how their data will be used and for what purposes. Having these rights does not extend to ownership of their data, at least not at this point. Data collected via learning analytics tools typically belongs to the tool's owner (Steiner et al., 2016). As with ethics and privacy definitions, issues of ownership are also evolving and that evolution is made more complicated given the context of higher education. Users are starting to be considered owners of data, as are higher education institutions. With individual users, higher education institutions, and learning analytics vendors all as potential owners of student-level data, "there arises the question of who the owner [of the data] actually is (Steiner et al., 2016, p. 80). When data ownership is left in question or is out of the hands of users, questions related to ethics and privacy come to the fore. Who decides what data are used, when they are used, and for what purpose? Answers to these ethical questions require thoughtful consideration of data ownership and its implications. Evolving laws, policies, and codes of practice are beginning to provide some guidance in this area and in the areas of security, access, and transparency, all of which engender increased trust in learning analytics.

Laws, Policies, and Codes of Practice

As with learning analytics, the associated laws, policies, and practices that exist on international, federal, state, and institutional levels that are focused on ethics and privacy related to educational data mining and analytics are sparse, but emerging. As societies and higher education institutions grapple with the promises, realities, and challenges of use of learning analytics, they are also reconsidering long-held laws, policies, and codes of practice related to ethical treatment of student data and privacy.

Laws and Regulations

The nascency of learning analytics means that associated laws and regulations exist at a beginning level of legal maturity, wherein current laws are not tailored to the existing needs and concerns of learning analytics technologies and do not provide clear interpretation or guidance on related ethics and privacy issues (Kay et al., 2012, p. 8). As such "legal systems are still at the early stages of commenting on privacy, ethics and data ownership" (Kay et al., 2012; Pardo & Siemens, 2014, p. 440). That being said, privacy and data ethics laws and regulations do exist, focusing mainly on research participant protections. Although not specific to learning analytics, they do provide a foundation of protection and guidance for both learning analytics developers and higher education administrators.

Current U.S. and international research laws have emerged from the Nuremberg Code (1964), Helsinki Declaration (1975), and Belmont Report (1978), which were the first and foundational documents that established a code of ethical conduct for researchers (Drachsler & Greller, 2016). Although these regulations were originally created to regulate medical research, a by-product was the creation of ethical committees and institutional review boards, whose missions include review of proposed research to ensure data subject protections (Drachsler & Greller, 2016).

Among specific laws related to protection of data subjects (identified individuals) in higher education, the European Commission (EC) Data Protection Directive states that "member states should ensure that legal frameworks allow higher education institutions to collect and analyse learning data" (Drachsler & Greller, 2016, p. 4). This directive works to provide both protection of an individual's data but also for the secure flow of the data across boundaries (Steiner et al., 2016). Cognizant of the importance of individual agency related to data collection, the directive also requires that students provide full and informed consent (Drachsler & Greller, p. 4), clear communication about what data are being collected and how data are being used, and student choice in anonymizing their data (Drachsler & Geller; Steiner et al., 2016). Although these aspects of the directive are useful to learning analytics, Drachsler and Greller argue that, given the repurposed and longitudinal nature of learning analytics, the directive is ultimately problematic, as it calls for data to be used within a specific time frame for a specific purpose.

Though not legal in nature, the Organisation for Economic Cooperation and Development (OECD) provides guidelines for "relevant source of basic principles when seeking guidance on how to deal with privacy issues in analytics technologies and other systems" (Steiner et al., 2016, p. 73). Based on European legal principles on privacy and individual protections, the OECD guidelines recommend limited, secure, relevant, and accountable data collection for specific purposes with data subject participation (Steiner et al., 2016). In 2013, the OECD guidelines were expanded to include additional data security protections across European boundaries (Steiner et al., 2016).

Similar laws and guidelines exist in the United States, most notably, the Family Educational Rights and Privacy Act, "which clarifies access to data sets (for example, access primarily for research, accountability, or institutional improvement) set against the need to maintain student privacy" (Slade & Prinsloo, 2013 p. 11). FERPA also provides protection related to identification and disclosure of data to third parties except when granted by the students themselves. This creates a tension in learning analytics systems that are founded on personalized data that are shared among stakeholders (Daries et al., 2014; Rubel & Jones, 2016). Yet, who stakeholders are is often ill defined by vendors and administrators and ill understood by users, as we have found in our work (Klein et al., in press). Importantly, as Rubel and Jones argue "if learning analytics live up to its promise and becomes a useful tool to predict academic (or other success), it is hard to imagine that other third parties (for example, insurance companies, creditors, especially potential employers would not seek to obtain information from learning analytics systems" (p. 150).

Given this potential, the need for protection of consent and informed choice by student data subjects is an imperative. The U.S. Federal Trade Commission's Fair Information Practice Principles (FIPP), which are based on the OECD guidelines, outlines the importance of informed consent, "allow[s] for different options regarding use of data, individuals' right[s] to check the accuracy and completeness of information, preventing unauthorized access, use and disclosure of data and provisions for enforcement and redress" (Slade & Prinsloo, 2013, p. 11; Steiner et al., 2016). The FIPP specifies concepts of fair information practice in the electronic marketplace, including giving users "notice/awareness" about their data; user "choice/consent" about how that data is used and collected; user ability to have "access/participation" with their data; vendor supported data "integrity/security;" and "enforcement/redress . . . through self-regulatory regimes, legislation . . . or government enforcement" (Steiner et al., 2016, p. 74).

Although the European and U.S. laws and regulations discussed here are not an exhaustive or internationally representative sample, they are among the most cited by learning analytics scholars as providing guidance for emerging legal and regulatory frameworks for learning analytics laws. These laws, in conjunction with various institutional policies and scholarly recommendations are creating an emerging ethical code of practice for learning analytics to protect the privacy of its users and integrity of its data.

Policies and Recommendations

As with various laws and regulations, policies related to data collection and data subject protections must be reconsidered given the emergence of learning analytics. By holistically reconsidering policies related to data, learning analytics developers and higher education institutions can create a unified approach, flexible to context, that addresses the use, dissemination, and protection of individual data. Policies are "the critical driving forces that underpin complex and systematic institutional problems and that shape perceptions of the nature of the problem(s) and acceptable solutions" (Macfayden et al., 2014, p. 22). Given the complexities of both learning analytics and higher education institutions and the evolving conceptions of ethics and privacy, clearly articulated policies that illuminate problems and provide solutions are vital.

Prinsloo and Slade (2013) argue that "realising the promise of learning analytics will require institutions to align their policies with national and international legislative frameworks; to consider the ethical issues inherent in the harvesting, use and dissemination of data and to ensure an enabling environment for adequate resourcing and integration of institutional support" (p. 1). This is a tall order for higher education institutions, as it requires a high level of coordination, collaboration, and goal alignment, actions that are difficult in siloed, loosely coupled, and complex college and university organizational structures (Kezar & Lester, 2009). Moreover, as with legal and regulatory matters, policies that speak specifically to the challenges and opportunities of learning analytics are just beginning to be defined and considered by higher education institutions (Prinsloo & Slade, 2013).

The importance of aligned and unified policies is that they can and "should provide not only an enabling environment or the optimal and ethical harvesting and use of data, but also clarify who benefits and under what conditions, establishes conditions for consent and the de-identification of data, and addresses issues of vulnerability and harm" (Prinsloo & Slade, 2013, p. 1). Unfortunately, they also argue that current policies are not adequate given the complex ethics related to learning analytics in higher education settings and the complexity and their various contexts (Prinsloo & Slade). That being said, there are policies in place on the national and international level that passively and actively address ethical and privacy issues related to data mining and learning analytics.

Prinsloo and Slade (2013) studied the various policies in place at two higher education institutions, Open University and Unisa. They found that these institutions, like most institutions in higher education, have a number of policies in place that were established to be in accordance with various laws and regulations related to the proprietary nature of data, data protection, and accessibility. Among these regulations are surveillance, privacy, conduct, ethical research, data security, fraud, records management, conditions of use, and social networking policies. However, none of the reviewed policies dealt specifically with the sort of student-level learning analytics data that could be analyzed, monitored, and acted upon within a learning analytics system (Prinsloo & Slade,). Overall, Prinsloo and Slade found that existing policies are "not always sufficient to address the specific ethical challenges in the harvest and analysis of big data in learning analytics" (p. 5).

Challenges in Practice

Not only are current policies, like current laws, not sufficient to address the challenges of learning analytics, but often individual users of learning analytics tools are unclear about how current policies, laws, and regulations affect their use of these tools. In a recent study focused on institutional opportunities and barriers related to use of learning analytics tools, we found that faculty and advising staff often shied away from using predictive data or specific notetaking components of those tools, for fear of violating FERPA rules and other campus policies (Klein et al., in press). Many of the faculty members and advisors we interviewed noted that they were uneasy about using note-taking components of learning analytics tools, as those notes are viewable by both the student and anyone with access to the student's file. Although FERPA rules allow for notetaking on institutional systems and sharing of information between colleagues, users were still wary. This wariness, arising from a concern that information would be taken out of context or would violate FERPA rules, creates a barrier to adoption of the learning analytics tool in use on the campus. Consequently, concern for student privacy and concern for violating federal and institutional policies inhibited full use of the learning analytics tool.

The existing uncertainty related to the policies, laws, and ethical guidelines that are meant to protect student privacy speak to the importance of having communications and training related to learning analytics use in higher education settings. Moreover, existing policies must be broadly embedded and clearly articulated by institutions so that individual users understand how to use and interpret learning analytics data and the associated components, like notetaking, related to these tools. In response to limited legal and policy frameworks and often limited understanding of how these laws and policies relate to learning analytics use in higher education, some vendors have responded to the growing legal focus on learning analytics by establishing principles for self-regulation (Beattie et al., 2014; Drachsler and Greller, 2016). Although self-regulation by vendors is a useful first step in creating ethical foundations to protect individual privacy, a code of practice with "common public standard[s] would be better" (Beattie et al., p. 424).

Emerging Codes of Practice

Current policies, initiatives, and practices provide a starting point for addressing ethics and privacy concerns. In the past few years, learning analytics scholars have begun to propose various frameworks and checklists to provide a more unified and aligned understanding of ethics and privacy issues and to suggest areas for ethical adherence to protect the privacy rights of learning analytics users (Beattie et al., 2014; Cormack, 2016; Drachsler & Greller, 2016; Pardo & Siemens, 2014; Sclater, 2016; Slade & Prinsloo, 2013; Steiner et al., 2016). Although these frameworks often differ in specific approach, there are themes that emerge across these frameworks for addressing ethics and privacy concerns. Among the most common themes are issues of transparency, security, trust, communication, data ownership and control, power and consent, and stewardship. In this section, we provide an overview of these frameworks and their themes and provide additional themes of importance, based on our own learning analytics research.

Historically, if learning analytics tool developers considered ethics and privacy at all, they did so with a privacy by policy-based mind-set. This mind-set provided for ethical and privacy considerations in response to or in compliance with established laws, regulations, and policies. There is movement, with the advent of various codes of practice and suggested frameworks, toward a privacy by design approach that constructs learning analytics tools from inception to implementation with ethical and privacy considerations integrated at all levels (Pardo & Siemens, 2016). Beattie et al. (2014) argue that a "Charter of Learner Data Rights" (p. 423) that is universal and integrates into its design issues related to the various concerns, considerations, laws, and policies related to learning analytics should be developed and applied as means to mitigate the potential harm of "creepy analytics" that have the potential to inflict harm (p. 421).

Current examples of frameworks that are striving to create universal and inclusive codes of practice include the Asilomar Charter of Learner Data Rights (Beattie et al., 2014), JISC's Code of Practice for Learning Analytics (Sclater & Bailey, 2015), the good practice guide for Safeguarding Student Learner Engagement (Cormack, 2016), the DELICATE checklist (Drachsler & Greller, 2016), LEA's Box (Steiner et al., 2016), and Slade and Prinsloo's (2013) Moral Practice Framework. What these codes of practice have in common is that they are beginning to create an understanding in the learning analytics field of the importance of having shared definitions and a holistic view of the various ethical and privacy concerns that permeate learning analytics from inception to implementation. These codes of practice are establishing the rules for an emergent discipline and industry in the areas of data privacy, purpose and ownership, consent, transparency and trust, access and control, accountability and assessment, quality, management, and security (Steiner et al., 2016).

As is evident in Slade and Prinsloo's (2013) moral practice framework, these codes of practice are important because, they argue, "education is primarily a moral practice, not a causal one. Therefore, learning analytics should function primarily as a moral practice resulting in understanding, rather than measuring" (p. 11). By creating learning analytics with ethics and privacy issues addressed throughout, learning analytics can have a greater impact on higher education (Slade & Prinsloo, 2013). The importance of considering issues of ethics and privacy by design is that it can help promote student trust, collaboration, and improved outcomes while minimizing the potential for bias, vulnerability, and harm.

Conclusion and Future Work

Learning analytics are part of the fabric of higher education, as these institutions work to improve institutional and individual performance and outcomes. Given the scale and nature of learning analytics data, careful consideration of ethics and privacy matters in the conception and design of learning analytics tools must exist in order to encourage user trust and adoption of these tools. This is a challenging task, as definitions of ethics and privacy and the laws, regulations, and codes of practice that have emerged to address these conceptions are constantly evolving.

Ultimately, the creation of a unified code of practice with a common language that is comprehensive enough to address privacy and ethics issues in details but flexible enough to be useful to the various contextual differences of countries, institutions, and needs is an important goal. Other important future work includes the continued development of laws and policies that not only address ethics and privacy but also are clearly articulated to learning analytics users. Finally, learning analytics algorithms and systems must become more transparent to engender greater understanding and trust of their potential or to allow for appropriate criticism when ethics, privacy, or bias tenets are violated.

As Willis and Pistilli (2014) note, "Although learning analytics might provide a pathway to efficiently helping students, they also involve critical decisions with far-reaching consequences" (p. 4). Multiple and varied decisions must be made, in collaboration with learning analytics users and with an understanding of the unique contexts of higher education institutions for effective ethics and privacy laws, policies, and codes of practice to be applied and used appropriately. Doing so will increase users' trust in these systems and their data.

Finally, users need to understand, in plain language, what they are giving up to receive access to various data systems on campus. As important, learning analytics developers and higher education administrators need to clearly communicate the benefits, parameters, and negotiation of data associated with these systems. Is the iris scan worth it; if it is only to save the institution the cost of a misused meal plan, how does that help the student? Does using predictive data help or hinder faculty pedagogy and student performance? Should advisors be actively taking notes on students if the data are perceived to violate privacy rules or if they fear data will be used inappropriately? Making understandable and relevant the ethics and privacy issues that users like Jamal, Anna, and Erica face so that they can collaborate with developers and administrators to improve future learning analytics systems is the vital crux of future work.

Recommendations for Moving Forward: Considerations of Organizational Complexity, Data Fidelity, and Future Research

A S THE PREVIOUS CHAPTERS illustrate, learning analytics has come to play an increasingly large role in higher education across a range of functions. The use of data for making decisions, at all levels of higher education institutions, is becoming common. Still, the potential from digital innovation has yet to be truly realized in terms of the substantial changes to higher education functioning and the barriers that exist, at multiple levels, to implementing these innovations. In this chapter, we use the framework proposed in the first chapter to look at how some of the issues associated with learning analytics in higher education can be mitigated and to consider the directions in which learning analytics needs to move for it to be transformational. The solutions, we believe, lie in thinking through the complexities of individual decision making, pedagogical change, organizational policies and practices, and data access, ethics, and privacy. As noted in prior chapters, data access, ethics, and privacy serve an essential role in developing, purchasing, implementing, and adopting learning analytics tools, whether you are an institutional administrator, faculty member, advisor, or student.

Learning Analytics in Higher Education: Model Considerations and Recommendations

Discussed throughout this text is the need to consider learning analytics more systemically as an interaction between organizational, technological, behavioral, and ethical considerations. In this section, we highlight some of the major concepts derived from the literature and offer specific recommendations of issues to consider in conversations and collaborations to build, adopt, or modify learning analytics tools.

Organizational Logic, Leadership, and Value

As stated previously, learning analytics readiness and capacity are an important consideration as institutions engage in conversations with internal stakeholders and with external vendors. From the technology infrastructure required to extract and analyze large amount of data to the skills of internal constituents to access and adoption of new tools and to organizational norms that guide individual behavior and place value on data as opposed to anecdotes, the state and capacity of an institution can determine the successful implementation of learning analytics tools. Although the literature on organizational readiness can provide an evaluation of an institution's capacity, what is missing from the research and recommendations on implementation is a broader set of considerations of institutional logics. More specifically, organizations need to conceptualize and strategize around a larger set of internal and external factors that help to frame, to make meaning of, and to motivate individuals to engage with and place a high value on the data visualized within learning analytics tools. Organizations also need to recognize opportunities to engage agency within the constraints in the larger social system.

Much evidence exists to support the notion that higher education institutions have succumbed to economic pressure and external pressures (Slaughter & Rhoades, 2004). Arguably, institutions of higher education have articulated external pressures as a need to engage in more capitalistic behaviors ranging from developing new forms of revenue through large endowment campaigns and partnerships to attention to institutional efficiency, such as increasing common metrics for student success (for example, graduation rates) (Alexander, 2000; Engle & Lynch, 2009). In addition, there is an increase in the use of formerly corporate terms, such as return on investment. Bastedo (2009) in a study of institutional logics found that campuses articulated external pressures as a need to differentiate missions from other competitor universities and to engage in more managerialism as a means to cope with the complexity of new institutional actions. Learning analytics and the many for-profit companies that are promoting new tools for purchase fall directly into the academic capitalist camp of behaviors. Moreover, they are a result of the interpretation by vendors and higher education institutions alike of the need for institutional efficiency. A cursory glance at websites of learning analytics tools as well as the reports coming from associated organizations, such as EDUCAUSE, reveals consistent promotion of learning analytics tools as a solution-based means to assist with college students' success including student retention and graduation.

Of note in this section on organizational considerations is the importance of leadership. Although leadership did not emerge in our focus groups studies, organizational change research often finds that supportive leadership plays a major role in successful change initiatives (Eckel & Kezar, 2003; Kezar, 2001; Kezar & Lester, 2009). In the case of learning analytics, leadership can play a role in removing structural and bureaucratic barriers (Arnold et al., 2014; Norris & Baer, 2013). For instance, the advisors in our study described a time-consuming process of needing to log on to multiple, as many as five, online systems to gather information on a single student to effectively advise him or her on future course schedules. At many institutions, student-to-advisor ratios are hundreds of students to a single advisor, resulting in advising appointments that last 15 or fewer minutes. During peak advising time, such as around course registration for the following semester, advisors are seeing students in 10 to 15 minute increments with no time in between appointments. Valuable time with students is then lost to cumbersome logon requirements of multiple systems. Leadership can play a role in remediating these technical issues by working across platforms and institutional units to create a single logon system. Although we are not suggesting this is an easy task, leadership has the authority to direct human resources and can negotiate across units and external vendors to facilitate these types of changes.

Additionally, leadership can play a role in facilitating meaning of and creating value for use of learning analytics tools. Another challenge noted in the literature (Dahlstrom et al., 2014) and our work is the ultimate decision by intended users to adopt learning analytics tools, whether they be advisors, faculty, or students. Data on Blackboard, which is historically a learning management system that has more recent embedded learning analytics components, notes that only 56% of faculty thoroughly engage in the system options (Dahlstrom et al., 2014). One prevailing issue is the ever-changing market for new learning analytics tools and the rapid change in the systems or the constant purchasing of new systems on a single college campus. Advisors in our study noted their growing frustration associated with the purchase of multiple systems in just a few years and that once they learn one system, it is discontinued and a new system is put in place with new learning requirements. There is also a lack of alignment and discourse between educational practice of advisors and faculty and tool development. All too often, faculty and advisors are simply informed of a new tool and given quick professional development focused solely on how to use the system or not even informed at all. Importantly, leadership can play a role in making connections between the overall mission and vision of the campus and the use of learning analytics tools. For example, campus leadership could articulate the mission of student success and the need to increase graduation rates. The new learning analytics tools could be framed as supporting and enabling higher graduation rates via the early warning systems, modeling future academic major course pathways, and signaling what students need and how to intervene to help them realize success. Much of the research on organizational change notes that leaders serve a meaning-making role, helping to facilitate decision making with overall institutional priorities (Amey, 2006; Eddy, 2012; Kezar, Carducci, & Contreras-McGavin, 2006). Learning analytics is an opportunity for leaders to facilitate strategic tool use to fulfill organizational initiatives.

Faculty and Advisor Input, Trust, and Engagement

In the third chapter, we argue that faculty and advisor adoption of learning analytics tools can be conceptualized in the context of the research on STEM faculty pedagogical change, specifically Austin's (2011) nested model of pedagogical change. Faculty and advisors consider pedagogical change, including technology adoption, at multiple levels and with factors related to their prior socialization experiences in graduate school, disciplinary norms, departmental contexts, and institutional factors, such as reward systems and leadership. Our research adds an additional element noting a relationship between organizational dynamics, technology infrastructure, and faculty and advisor educational philosophy and trust.

Specific to learning analytics tools that is not directly relevant to Austin's model of STEM pedagogy change is technology infrastructure and institutional factors. In agreement with the literature on faculty adoption of technology (as well as other studies on adoption) not in a higher education setting, our findings, specific to higher education, indicate that barriers to adoption exist for faculty include a lack of accuracy, quality, and trustworthiness of data related to learning analytics tools and a lack of communication and training in bifurcated or closed systems. Many of these issues are related to the technical aspects of tools—institutional collection of data to ensure quality, a lack of communication on tool acquisition and improvements, and barriers to ease of use, such as access to the tools. Underlying many of these barriers is an issue of trust. Hora et al. (2014) found that a barrier for faculty adoption of tools is perception of the quality of data. When prior data collected and analyzed at an institution are poor or there is a perception that institutional data are lacking in quality because of collection or data storage and retrieval issues, any tool built using those data is circumspect and lacks trust.

Further complicating these issues is the refinement process that tools must complete after being deployed to users. In our research, tools were often deployed to the entire campus after a short pilot phase wherein a few individuals had an opportunity to engage the tool to identify any bugs—broken links, missing data, and so on—and provide feedback on various tool components. When more users began to use the tool in introductory workshops and in everyday practice, even more issues were uncovered. An example of these issues is a learning analytics tool that allowed for reports to be run based on student characteristics. An advisor wanted to run a report on all the student athletes in her major, as she has anecdotally watched student athletes struggle academically in the past. Unfortunately, the data made available to the company managing the learning analytics tool did not include "athlete" as a variable, which made this report impossible to run. The result was that this advisor and many others in our study discontinued use of the tool once one error was found. Mistrust of data by users was easy to occur when components went wrong, which made gaining trust much more challenging.

The literature on technology adoption adds a new understanding of individual interpretation of elements of data visualization (Dawson et al., 2008); simply, more straightforward and relevant data visualized in an easy-to-read manner led to greater levels of trust and more consistency in tool adoption. Underlying these concerns is a question of relevance, a finding highlighted in our studies of learning analytics. Often, institutions purchase a learning analytics tool without any input from users whether they be faculty, advisors, or students. Without consultation during the design, acquisition, and implementation stages, users are not given an opportunity to evaluate the usefulness of the tool and to begin to consider how to adopt it into current professional practices.

To attempt to create more trust, three recommendations are important: (a) include users in the design and development of learning analytics tools, (b) have longer and more intense pilot periods with feedback from multiple stakeholders, and (c) create comprehensive and intensive training, communication, and marketing campaigns on issues raised and, more important, when they are resolved. For the first recommendation, learning analytics tool developers and vendors should not just seek input from intended users but also include those users in the design process. Our research consistently noted that faculty and advisors felt aspects of the tools were unhelpful to their practice (Klein et al., 2016a, 2016b). Moreover, advisors and faculty have specific educational philosophies and individually proven practices that may or may not align with the tools. Faculty and advisors are often given opportunities to engage in workshops on *how* to use the tools but not *why* they should use the tools and no discussion of how the tools integrate into their education philosophies. For example, many advisors in our focus groups expressed a developmental advising philosophy with a deep commitment to an interpersonal approach to advising. Advisors noted that you often need to see the interpersonal communication with students to really gauge their academic and personal interests and to intervene if issues are apparent. Learning analytics tools are often touted as replacements for high-touch advising, which is in direct contrast to the philosophies of advisors. Institutions need to develop workshops and learning experiences that are less focused on how to use the tool, such as how to run a report or which links to click, and more on how to integrate it into advisor and faculty current practice and philosophies. For example, a workshop may begin with writing and discussion of educational philosophies with further discussion on where tools can be integrate aligned with these values. Tools can help advisors with large caseloads by creating reports on groups or individual students to target for in-person interventions. They can also help to create if–then analyses to respond to student queries about changing academic majors. The articulation of alignment between tools and practice needs to continue beyond the one-time workshop and into the advising units and faculty academic departments. Therefore, workshops for department chairs and unit managers to support advisors and faculty are needed.

For the second recommendation, once a tool has been designed, stakeholders from across campus to include those who provide the data (institutional research offices), those who use the data (faculty and advisors), and the unit managers and department chairs and others (advising center directors, for example) who promote user engagement with the tool need to be part of the pilot process to provide feedback for and garner long-term investment in and development of the tool. If possible, these groups need to be engaged in a collaborative way to help resolve complex concerns. In the example of the advisor who wanted to target student athletes, having institutional research office representatives who could have facilitated creating a data file with this information, which would then be fed back into the tool, would have been an important connection for improving tool functionality and increasing user trust. Task forces, committees, and feedback sessions are just a few ways to create more collaborative spaces.

For the third recommendation, feedback loops need to be in place to allow users and managers to provide quick and timely criticism on tool elements. This could be in the form of a dedicated email address, discussion forums, town halls, and reports. Professional development and learning analytics tool training sessions could also be used to provide for this feedback and to educate the campus community of the existence and potential uses of learning analytics tools. This speaks to the need for communications plans that pay attention to the needs of potential users by addressing learning analytics tools' potential and challenges. Early-adopter faculty proselytizers as critical advocates for these tools can be a key component to increasing visibility for potential users. Most important, communications plans should include mechanisms that ensure that the users providing the feedback must also receive a response with resolved issues being communicated to the campus writ large. For example, the issues of student athlete reports could be communicated directly back to that one advisor and an email (including other campus-based communication forums) could be sent to the entire campus making other users aware of the new student athlete reports available.

College Student Interpretation of and Context for Data

The research on college students and learning analytics is thin. Minus the few studies that examine college student behavior, such as the Marist College study and a few other reports from the Purdue Course Signals Project (Arnold & Pistilli, 2012; Jayaprakesh et al., 2014), little is known about how students engage in, making meaning of, and change behaviors based on exposure to learning analytics tools. The research from our work does provide some evidence previously unknown, namely, that the visualizations that students experience via use of these tools can affect student use and subsequent action.

Results from our work indicate that students are aware of and use a variety of educational technology tools over the course of their college careers (Klein et al., 2017). Although they do not differentiate between tools that are learning analytics informed or always understand how their data are being mined via these tools, students find them useful for specific tasks, like fulfilling course assignments and tracking grades. They deem the data provided in these tools and their visualizations useful in assessing and reflecting upon their academic coursework and progress and in acting as an academic recordkeeping system. However, this assessment and recordkeeping ability is constrained when faculty do not use these systems; when institutions do not provide timely, accurate, or integrated informational updates; and when visualizations are provided with confusing data, unclear language, or without context.

Without context students felt that their data were being provided to them in a vacuum, which disconnected them from understanding how those data connected to their course performance and degree progress. Many learning analytics tool performance and progress visualizations use color signals to indicate performance status. Although this seems like a straightforward means of communicating student performance, many of the students we queried noted that they found the color alone was not a helpful indicator of their progress. Rather, they wanted to understand the meanings behind the various colors and how that color signal situated them against their peers' progress and performance in the course. Students argued that visualizations and interventions provided without context are likely to be ignored or questioned by students. They also argued that a lack of context might encourage them to act in opposition to the intended intervention. Students we interviewed felt intervention emails often seemed too automated, even when those emails were from faculty and specific to their performance. Despite their intended support interventions are designed to provide, students do not always react to those communications as expected. Messages of support are often not trusted or deemed worthy of attention.

When there is an absence of alignment, context, and personalization, trust in these tools falters. This mistrust is compounded when there is no relationship between the student and their faculty. Students argued that they needed to trust their faculty before they would fully trust a tool used to deliver course performance data. The relationships students build with their faculty affect their perceptions of data those faculty and learning analytics tools communicate to them. Finally, although students do not differentiate between data that are based on analytics and those that are not, they were skeptical of data that are predictive in nature and chafed at the idea of an algorithm suggesting a future course of action based on past performance. Despite the positively intended purpose, predictive data, or data that are unclear, automated, or untrusted, affect students' use, perceptions, and behaviors regarding learning analytics data.

In terms of recommendations, what our research and that of others indicates is a need to more broadly understand the technological skills and engagement of college students. All too often the common discourse is that newer generations, beginning with millennials, are tech savvy relying on cell phones and other technologies as the primary forms of communication. In fact, EDUCAUSE identified a digital divide where access to technology and skills development is more diverse (Brown, Dehoney, & Millichap, 2015). Colleges and universities need to be more cognizant of the fact that not all students have quick and easy access to computers and cell phones nor do they have the skills to engage in and make meaning of learning analytics. Simply, a common message is that students need opportunities to learn how to access, engage in, and integrate learning analytics into their collegiate experience. One recommendation is for faculty to integrate learning analytics into their courses with identified learning outcomes on technology skills. An instructor, for example, could review the learning analytics tools the first day of class, create expectations tied to participation points for accessing the tools, describe any early warning systems, and then be clear about how the instructor will engage the tool, such as posting grades and expecting responses to emails indicating a drop in grades or engagement. Any efforts by faculty also need to be supported via the organizational considerations noted earlier in this chapter.

Because students make important decisions related to their coursework and degree progress based on their interactions with learning analytics tools, more work needs to be done to understand how students interpret and internalize data, particularly predictive data. Many of the recommendations specific to learning analytics tools for faculty and advisors are relevant to student use as well. As with faculty and advisors, students should be involved in the creation, design, development, and implementation of these tools on campus. As a part of our work, we intentionally included undergraduate researchers to help us design learning analytics tools visualization prototypes that their peers could react to. By far, students reacted more positively to the peer-created prototypes than to existing tools on the market. This is, according to participating students, because those tools spoke their language and met their needs. Students were generally more open to tools that aligned with their needs and their ways of being.

Thus, another recommendation is for learning analytics vendors and institutions to think, prior to implementation, of how the tools will be used by students on the ground. Tools that allow students to seamlessly access real-time data are more likely to be trusted and used by students. Again, as with faculty and advisors, students who encountered difficult-to-use tools, difficult-to-understand visualizations, or tools that provided limited or incorrect data were less likely to be used in the future (unless required by faculty). It is important for learning analytics tools to provide student users with information they can trust and act upon. Yet, learning analytics tools alone are not a magic bullet for student retention and completion. Our work indicates that no matter how good the data or how well intentioned the intervention, human interaction is foundational to student retention and completion. Students noted time and again that although receiving their data is useful, they need to trust where those data come from in order to trust the data. However, this trust requires a relationship between faculty, advisors, and students. Our final recommendation is to encourage the use of learning analytics as a tool for faculty and advisors to continue conversations with their students about their performance and progress and to discourage administrative actions that might take relationship building out of the equation by focusing on the innovation alone. Students need guidance in making meaning of their data and of the visualizations they receive through learning analytics tools. Faculty and advisors can provide that frontline meaning making but only if they receive, as we recommended earlier, professional development to help them develop an understanding of these tools and their impacts.

Ethics and Privacy: Transparency and Ownership

In the fourth chapter, we provided an overview of issues related to ethics and privacy, issues that are embedded in learning analytics tools from development to deployment to use and action and that affect all user of learning analytics technologies. As with other learning analytics-associated studies, the literature on ethics and privacy is emergent. Although there have been a number of scholarly papers associated with conceptions, definitions, and codes of ethics related to ethics and privacy in the field of learning analytics (Drachsler et al., 2015; Ferguson et al., 2016; Pardo & Siemens, 2014; Prinsloo & Slade, 2015; Rubel & Jones, 2016; Sclater, 2016; Slade & Prinsloo, 2013, 2015; Steiner et al., 2016; Swenson, 2014; Willis, 2014; Willis & Pistilli, 2014), few actual studies on ethics and privacy have been conducted. Those studies that do focus on ethics and privacy are usually focused on use and protection of student-level data.

The preliminary work that has been done related to ethics and privacy has been to establish a shared understanding of these concepts and to define them in relation to higher education data and to provide a similar template for communicating the importance of this area of future research by outlining historical views of ethics and privacy, offering definitions and proofs of concept, laying out existing and relevant laws and regulations, and illustrating aspects of emerging promising practices and guidelines.

Given the unique privacy issues related to use of student data in higher education, there are unique challenges associated with ensuring the ethical use and protection of the data by both learning analytics vendors and higher education institutions. The necessity for user data to be protected requires that vendors and institutions act from an ethical standpoint. Although many, and we would argue the majority of vendors and institutions, act from a well-intentioned place, as we discussed previously, matters of ethics and privacy are often not considered in the development and implementation of learning analytics tools. Moreover, vendors and institutions often have not clearly articulated what data are being mined via learning analytics tools, where the data are held, how they are used, what algorithmic components are used to establish interventions, and perhaps most important, who owns data that have been mined from learning analytics tools used in higher education. The issue of ownership is tied to agency. Across the scholarly papers associated with ethics and agency, scholars call for the active inclusion of users in decisions related to use of their data. Although their focus is often on student data, given that faculty and advising staff are also frequent users of data systems in higher education, they should be included in considerations of agency as they relate to learning analytics data. Moreover, institutions should think about data ownership and protection at the institutional level.

As referenced in the beginning of this chapter, higher education institutions are increasingly engaging with technology vendors that are encouraging use of learning analytics tools to address retention and completion problems. We have noted the promise of these tools; however, incorporation of these tools into the higher education landscape requires that institutions think of data ownership beyond the individual level. Learning analytics tools are touted as a means to help organizations to meet their duties to care for and to act on behalf of their students. However, it is not yet clear what impact these tools are having on higher education institutions and their students. Moreover, the lack of transparency of these proprietary tools means that it is impossible to understand the algorithmic basis upon which data-driven decisions that emerge from tool use are based. Lack of transparency is a significant issue related to ethics and privacy that must be addressed as future learning analytics tools are developed for use in higher education.

Equally important to ethics and privacy are issues of data ownership. Whether students have ownership of their data, it is equally unclear if institutions do. Institutions often purchase tools, like learning analytics technologies, with no clear articulation of who owns the data being collected via those tools. For higher education institutions, this is problematic on a number of fronts. Most important, it potentially dances on the line of FERPA violations by allowing nondirectory student information to be shared with individuals and corporations beyond the bounds of the university. But, it also gives over a wealth of data and information to a third party and further opens higher education to the influence and insertion of outside forces. We argue that having clearly articulated agreements between vendors and institutions, in addition to the codes of practice that are currently being proposed by members of the learning analytics community, is an important step in ensuring an ethical approach to protecting user privacy.

Data Concerns and Recommendations

Learning analytics tools are complex to integrate into higher education practice because of organizational norms and cultures as well as faculty, advisor, and student behaviors and beliefs. Before any of these issues are a consideration, data must be available and of a high quality to build the tools. Simply, learning analytics tools cannot exist without data. And, like other issues, data come with their own set of complexities. In this section, we outline some of the major concerns and recommendations related to data.

Data Access, Provenance, and Fidelity

The fundamental input to any analytical system is data, or information, more broadly, and the challenges for learning analytics often stem from this. The first issue is availability of and access to data. As digitization of systems and devices increases, data are becoming more omnipresent, but for proper use, the data need to be accessible to users. Second, the data provenance needs to be clear. Where did the data come from? For this, and for better description of data, useful metadata is required. Finally, for analytical impact, multiple data streams need to be aligned, and for this to take place, data creation needs to be similar. Once the data stream is in place, data sharing is paramount for scaling up the process of research and of impact. Overall, the community needs federated data sets that allow researchers as well as application developers to be able to learn from data. Only through long-term efforts can data fidelity be established. Not all data are good or useful but it is hard to know upfront which data are useful. Without that knowledge, the fidelity of analysis is low and therefore it is hard to trust decisions based on that analysis.

To improve the availability of data across its systems, a higher education institution needs to build data capacity across all information technology systems implemented at the institution. The challenge that many institutions need to overcome regarding this is the presence of legacy systems with different databases at the back end. A common task force with the requisite expertise that can evaluate what exists and how it can be made to work together is the first step. In some instances, new systems or at least more current versions of the system might need to be installed.

Use-Case/Scenario-Based Design of Systems

The access to data is a good first step but in conjunction with that the design of analytical systems also requires an in-depth understanding of users and the scenarios they face. Use-case design and scenario-driven design are both useful methodologies that allow designers to gain contextual understanding of how users perform their work. This requires not just the ability to use flashy design software but ability to conduct naturalistic observations and interviews with potential users. The overall process is often time consuming and therefore designers often resort to shortcuts. This is a primary reason that the systems that are designed lack usability and, more important, usefulness to potential users. Undertaking design of systems within an institution is not an easy task but many communities have expertise in this area. Many higher education institutions have an in-house design team that continually interacts with stakeholders—student, faculty administrators, staff—to better understand their needs and design and tailor applications for them.

Work Practice Integration of Systems

From a work practice perspective, the creation and implementation of systems that are usable and useful still require the proper strategy for how the systems are integrated within the existing work practices of users. In the event that new work practices have to be established, as is often the case, then training and translation of existing practices to new ones are needed. Currently, the work practices of faculty, for instance, when it comes to research and teaching functions are disjointed. For all practical purposes, these two functions are different elements bundled within the same job. Learning analytics, for most faculty members, are related to the teaching function but not necessarily to research. In such a context, what would it take to get faculty to change their teaching work practices? What is the reward structure like? Even if faculty are fully on board with improving student learning, what kind of time and resource investment is needed? Technological systems also suffer from the problem that rewards—at a macro level and micro level—are far into the future, and therefore without the immediate return, motivating users to change practices they are comfortable with is hard.

Personalized Information for Stakeholders

Many users of these analytic systems have capabilities to be personalized to some degree but future systems, especially those targeting students need a higher level of personalization. This means that at some level, some of the data have to come from the individual, and there are additional privacy and trust issues with such systems. But to be truly effective in supporting learning, the systems need to move from generic data to personal data and also data about the user's or learner's ambience. The future of personalization is hard to predict, but given the increased ambient computing, it is certainly on the rise. How can we develop systems that take into account both cognitive and affective aspects of learning? How do we leverage data coming from devices, biomarkers, a learning system, and so on, to effectively create a personalized learning environment? How crucial is such a system and what are the learning gains? These are all critical questions that need to be addressed.

Use-Inspired Research in Pasteur's Quadrant: Integrated Education, Research, and Advising

Research on education and learning, and in learning analytics, operates in what Donald Stokes (2011) identified as the Pasteur's Quadrant—the use-inspired research paradigm as opposed to fully theoretical or fully practical research. The idea from a research perspective is to create new knowledge and improve existing knowledge but also ensure that the knowledge generated is applicable to problems at hand. This, currently, is a problem within the research community as many researchers, those from a computer science background, are largely interested in developing new algorithms or techniques using learning-related data and not necessarily working toward improving learning. On the other hand, researchers from a higher education, learning sciences, or educational psychology background are more interested in improving education and learning but not necessarily driven by creating new computation-related knowledge. Consequently, there is a greater need for more interdisciplinary collaboration that is catalyzed by scholars who can bring these communities together. The other community that needs to be involved is the learning technology specialists on campus who are often responsible for the technology rollout and ensuring its effectiveness.

Privacy, Accountability, Transparency, Security, and Trust

As stated previously, it is impossible to predict what the future of data looks like but there is no doubt that issues of security, transparency, and accountability will become paramount. Users differ in their perceptions of how they want their data to be used, but it is imperative that there is transparency as without that it is hard for learners to trust the information they are getting based on those data. Privacy norms seem to be shifting with time and users of digital devices and systems are becoming increasingly comfortable about sharing their information. This is an important development within the context of learning analytics, because at this point, most of the interventions to support student learning are at the level of faculty or advisor. It is quite plausible to imagine a scenario where peers might be more useful intermediaries of learning or external coaches, hired privately by students. Should or could they get the same access as faculty and advisors?

Suggestions for Future Research

As noted, the research on learning analytics in higher education is in its infancy. Many basic research questions remain to fully understand the impact of learning analytics in higher education practice. These questions range from how to implement learning analytics, what impact they have, and how students and others make meaning of them. Although not exhaustive, we offer several areas for future research.

Quasiexperimental Designs of Intervention Impacts

In 2014, Marist College completed a small-scale study on the student behavioral response to methods that results from an early warning system (Jayaprakesh et al., 2014). An email was sent to students who were in danger of failing a course, noting different actions the student could take to try to successfully complete the course. Using a control group of students in the same course who did not receive the email, the results from the study found that students who received the email were more likely to withdraw from the course. The intention was not for students to withdraw, thus paying for the course and not receiving course credit toward their major, but to take one or more of the suggestions (including meeting with their professor) and pass the course. There are very few studies that identify the impact of early warning systems or other learning analytic tools on college student behavior and success. Several new studies are needed to identify the impact, particularly any unintended harm, resulting from communication and use of different learning analytic tools. First, more experiential or quasiexperimental studies are needed similar to the Marist College study but expanding beyond early warning system emails to include how students make meaning of and conceptualize the data being presented in learning analytics tools and the subsequent actions they may take based on those data.

Modeling Student Engagement

For the last few decades, research (Kuh, 2001, 2003, 2008; Kuh, Kinzie, Shuh, & Whitt, 2011) has conclusively identified a series of student engagement measures that predict college student success. With studies across institutional types, geographic locations, and different student demographic, academic and social engagement contributes to college student semester-to-semester retention and graduation. These studies, however, are all self-report and some researchers (Campbell & Cabrera, 2011; Dowd, Sawatzky, & Korn, 2011; Lester, Brown Leonard, & Mathias, 2013; Porter & Umbach, 2006) have called into question the efficacy of the National Survey of Student

Engagement (NSSE) results, particularly the limitations with diverse student populations. For example, Lester et al. (2013) found in a qualitative study that adult transfer students conceptualize social engagement and support outside of the context of the college, preferring support within their families and communities. The availability of big educational data can provide a platform to reimagine student engagement measures by eliminating self-report data. For example, a study at Dartmouth used a smartphone sensing application to capture data on mental health outcomes for college students, such as level of stress, sleep patterns, and conversation levels (Wang et al., 2014). These data collected on a large scale can help to quantify some of the classic engagement measures in higher education research.

Modeling and Visualizing Student Learning Preferences and Prior Learning Outcomes

Another area ripe for additional research is in modeling student learning preferences. The beliefs around student learning styles has been largely debunked, but there is still an acknowledgment that students tend to have preferred ways to learn (Coffield, Mosely, & Hall, 2004; Willingham, Hughes, & Dobolyi, 2015). In addition, there is plenty of evidence in science and engineering education to support the efficacy of active learning in college classrooms. Research, however, has yet to fully uncover how to measure learning preferences.

A potential value of learning analytics tools for faculty is the ability to know more about students before entering the first course meeting, such as learning preferences, level of competency (for example, beginning, intermediate, or advanced) in learning outcomes, academic major, and prior academic success overall. This type of data would allow faculty to engage in more intense and differentiated planning to use each hour of course time effectively and efficiently. To have a tool with these data requires several new areas of research. First and as noted previously, more research is needed on student learning preferences that operationalizes concepts such as those in Bloom's Taxonomy (Bloom & Krathwohl, 1956; Krathwohl, 2002). Although it is a useful taxonomy to frame different levels of student thinking, there are no measures empirically verified or methodologies that could be integrated into learning analytics tools. Second, there needs to be more research on measuring student learning outcomes. To date, the research is often more qualitative in nature, applying rubrics and creating student portfolios to demonstrate application of concepts, such as critical thinking. Integration into learning analytics tools will require more systematic review of student learning outcomes, agreement on appropriate measurements and how to quantify those measures. This is no small task as the work would likely need to be done on the department, or academic program, level.

Development of these tools could also play a role in faculty teaching evaluation. Several recent studies provide solid evidence of the lack of efficacy of student course evaluations (Adams & Umbach, 2012; Beleche, Fairris, & Marks, 2012; Goos & Salomons, 2016; Treischl & Wolbring, 2017; Wolbring & Treischl, 2016). Carl Wieman's (2015, 2017) work has several new evaluation tools in place that help to address teaching practices and a few projects, such as one at University of Colorado (Lester, Klein, Rangwala, & Johri, in press), are developing more integrated online systems more akin to electronic portfolios for teaching evaluation. Importantly, more work is currently being done to move beyond simple self-report measures of biased student evaluations. Future research is needed to determine how to successfully and purposefully integrate learning analytics into evaluation that takes into account faculty effort, innovation, and, most important, rewards. New studies could focus on the development and implementation of faculty portfolio tools that document faculty work around teaching innovations, new forms of student assessment, and reflective documents to reveal the actual work required to redesign courses and engage in active learning. Moreover, learning analytics could be integrated to allow for faculty to engage in real-time reflection and adjustments also documenting the workload of engagement in teaching practices.

Developing Ethical Codes of Practice and Use

As stated previously, more work needs to be done to develop comprehensive and agreed-upon ethical codes of practice and best practices for ethical use of learning analytics tools and protection of user privacy. A number of promising codes have been developed over the past decade, with Australia and countries in Europe taking the lead. Similarly, in Europe, Australia, and the United States, laws, legal frameworks, and guidelines have been developed that are establishing boundaries for ethical use of data and privacy protections. However, a comprehensive and agreed-upon set of codes and legal frameworks has yet to be established. Although this may ultimately be impossible, future work should include attempts to provide seamless guidelines related to learning analytics data collection and use.

Beyond the development of legal frameworks, ethical codes of practice and best practices for protecting learning analytics tool users' privacy, inquiry into issues of user agency, data access and protections, and algorithmic bias are ripe for further study. It is important to understand what faculty, advisor, and student users know about what data are being collected about them and how the data are used, the boundaries of their agency within that collection and use (how much they want to control about what is collected and shared about them), and the institutional implications of not providing the transparency necessary for informed agentic action by learning analytics tool users.

Speaking of transparency, it is often impossible to understand what impact learning analytics tools will have if the algorithms underlying them are not transparent. Understanding which variables can affect student success is vital to providing a duty of care. As such, learning analytics tool developers have an ethical obligation to provide transparent development and evaluation of their tools. We understand that this is antithetical to many of the current models on the market, which are embedded in an academic capitalistic system that requires proprietary action. However, we argue that given the importance of student retention and completion and given education's duty to care and to act, these tools should be open source, with components that are openly available for use, interrogation, and future research.

The benefit of doing more work in the area of best practices, codes of practice, legal framework, user agency, and transparency is that it has the potential to increase trust and use of learning analytics tools. These issues as they relate to ethics and to privacy should not be viewed as a barrier but rather can be viewed as potential levers for increased use and adoption. It is the responsibility of vendors and higher education institutions alike to approach ethics and privacy work with a mental model that is rooted in a sense of possibility rather than constraint.

Conclusion

Learning analytics in higher education has much potential and the market for such tools is growing. Institutions of higher education need to take caution when discussing the purchase, development, or implementation of such tools as they encounter the very forces that shape higher education. In this monograph, we outlined a multifaceted model that takes into account the literature on technology adoption, data visualization, organizational change, and faculty pedagogy change to provide new directions for research and considerations for practitioners currently investing or already invested in learning analytics.

Resources

APEREO LEARNING ANALYTICS INITIATIVE, https://www.apereo.org/communities/learning-analytics-initiative: "The Apereo Learning Analytics Initiative (LAI) aims to accelerate the operationalization of Learning Analytics software and frameworks, support the validation of analytics pilots across institutions, and work together so as to avoid duplication where possible."

Association for Computing Machinery (ACM), http://www.acm.org/: "ACM brings together computing educators, researchers, and professionals to inspire dialogue, share resources, and address the field's challenges. As the world's largest computing society, ACM strengthens the profession's collective voice through strong leadership, promotion of the highest standards, and recognition of technical excellence. ACM supports the professional growth of its members by providing opportunities for life-long learning, career development, and professional networking."

Centre for Educational Technology, Interoperability and Standards (CETIS), http://jisc.cetis.ac.uk/: "JISC CETIS is an Innovation Support Centre advising UK further and higher education on the strategic, technical and pedagogical implications of educational technology and standards. It also provides strategic advice to JISC, supports its innovation programmes, and represents JISC on international standardisation initiatives. It supports the wider educational community by organising meetings, workshops and conferences and offers daily comment and analysis on current developments in educational technology through its website. Through an iterative cycle of horizon scanning, publications, and community engagement, JISC CETIS fulfils a crucial role in linking innovative technological and standards developments with JISC programme scoping, funding and management. Involvement in relevant communities of practice and standards bodies, both nationally and internationally, is key in supporting these activities."

EDUCAUSE, https://www.EDUCAUSE.edu: EDUCAUSE helps those who lead, manage, and use information technology to shape strategic decisions at every level. EDUCAUSE actively engages with colleges and universities, corporations, foundations, government, and other nonprofit organizations to further the mission of transforming higher education through the use of information technology.

European Distance and E-Learning Network (EDEN), http://www.eden-online.org/: "The European Distance and E-Learning Network exists to share knowledge and improve understanding amongst professionals in distance and e-learning and to promote policy and practice across the whole of Europe and beyond."

JISC Effective Learning Analytics, https://analytics.jiscinvolve.org/wp/category/network/: "The Effective Learning Analytics challenge is about using data and analytics to support students; improving satisfaction, retention and graduation rates."

Journal of Learning Analytics, http://learning-analytics.info/: The *Journal of Learning Analytics* is a peer-reviewed, open-access journal, disseminating the highest quality research in the field. The journal is the official publication of the Society for Learning Analytics Research (SoLAR).

Learning Analytics & Knowledge Conferences, http://lak17.solaresearch.org/: Official conferences for the Society of Learning Analytics Research.

Learning Analytics & Knowledge (LAK) Dataset & Challenge, http://lak.linkededucation.org/: "The LAK Dataset makes publicly available machine-readable versions of research sources from the Learning Analytics and Educational Data Mining communities, where the main goal is to facilitate research, analysis and smart explorative applications. This website provides a home for the LAK Dataset as well as the associated LAK Data Challenge and contains the latest information about the data itself as well as latest calls and updates related to the LAK Data Challenges."

Learning Analytics Community Exchange (LACE), http://www.laceproject.eu/: "The Learning Analytics Community Exchange was an EU funded project in the 7th Framework Programme involving nine partners from across Europe. LACE partners are passionate about the opportunities afforded by current and future views of learning analytics (LA) and educational data mining (EDM) but we were concerned about missed opportunities and failing to realise value. The project aimed to integrate communities working on LA and EDM from schools, workplace and universities by sharing effective solutions to real problems."

Society of Learning Analytics Research (SOLAR), https://solaresearch.org: "The Society for Learning Analytics Research (SoLAR) is an interdisciplinary network of leading international researchers who are exploring the role and impact of analytics on teaching, learning, training and development. SoLAR has been active in organizing the International Conference on Learning Analytics & Knowledge (LAK) and the Learning Analytics Summer Institute (LASI), launching multiple initiatives to support collaborative and open research around learning analytics, promoting the publication and dissemination of learning analytics research, and advising and consulting with state, provincial, and national governments."

SOLAR News & Newsletters: https://solaresearch.org/stay-informed/signup/news-archive/

Supporting Higher Education in Learning Analytics (SHEILA) Project, http://sheilaproject.eu/: "To assist European universities to become more mature users and custodians of digital data about their students as they learn online, the SHEILA project will build a policy development framework that promotes formative assessment and personalized learning, by taking advantage of direct engagement of stakeholders in the development process."

U.S. Department of Education Office of Educational Technology: https://tech.ed.gov/learning-analytics/: "The U.S. Department of Education Office of Educational Technology (OET) develops national educational technology policy and establishes the vision for how technology can be used to transform teaching and learning and how to make everywhere, all-the-time learning possible for early learners through K–12, higher education, and adult education."

References

Adams, M. J., & Umbach, P. D. (2012). Nonresponse and online student evaluations of teaching: Understanding the influence of salience, fatigue, and academic environments. *Research in Higher Education*, *53*(5), 576–591.

Adelman, C., Ewell, P., Gaston, P., & Geary Schneider, C. (2014). *Degree qualifications profile*. Indianapolis, IN: Lumina Foundation.

Alexander, F. K. (2000). The changing face of accountability: Monitoring and assessing institutional performance in higher education. *Journal of Higher Education*, *71*(4), 411–431.

Ali, L., Hatala, M., Gašević, D., & Jovanović, J. (2012). A qualitative evaluation of evolution of a learning analytics tool. *Computers & Education*, *58*(1), 470–489.

Almatrafi, O., Rangwala, H., Johri, A., & Lester, J. (2016, February). Using learning analytics to trace academic trajectories of CS and IT students to better understanding successful pathways to graduation. *Proceedings of the 47th ACM Technical Symposium on Computing Science Education*. New York, NY: Association of Computing Machinery, 691.

Amey, M. J. (1999). Faculty culture and college life: Reshaping incentives toward student outcomes. In J. D. Toma & A. J. Kezar (Eds.), *New directions for higher education: No, 105. Reconceptualizing the collegiate ideal* (pp. 59–69). San Francisco, CA: Jossey-Bass.

Andrejevic, M. (2011). Social network exploitation. In Z. Papacharissi (Ed.), *A networked self: Identity, community, and culture on social network sites* (pp. 82–101). New York, NY: Routledge.

Appleby, D. C. (2008). Advising as teaching and learning. *Academic Advising: A Comprehensive Handbook*, *2*, 85–102.

Arnold, K. E., Lonn, S., & Pistilli, M. D. (2014). An exercise in institutional reflection: The learning analytics readiness instrument (LARI). *Proceedings of the Fourth International Conference on Learning Analytics and Knowledge*. New York, NY: Association of Computing Machinery, 163–167.

Arnold, K. E., & Pistilli, M. D. (2012). Course signals at Purdue: Using learning analytics to increase student success. *Proceedings of the Second International Conference on Learning Analytics and Knowledge.* New York, NY: Association of Computing Machinery, 267–270.

Arroway, P., Morgan, G., O'Keefe, M., & Yanosky, R. (2016). *Learning analytics in higher education (Research report).* Louisville, CO: ECAR. Retrieved from https://library.EDUCAUSE.edu/˜/media/files/library/2016/2/ers1504la.pdf

Astin, A. W. (1993). *What matters in college: Four critical years revisited.* San Francisco, CA: Jossey-Bass.

Austin, A. E. (2003). Creating a bridge to the future: Preparing new faculty to face changing expectations in a shifting context. *Review of Higher Education, 26*(2), 119–144.

Austin, A. E. (2011). *Promoting evidence-based change in undergraduate science education.* Paper commissioned by the National Academies National Research Council. Retrieved from http://tidemarkinstitute.org/sites/default/files/documents/Use%20of%20Evidence%20in%20Changinge%20Undergraduate%20Science%20Education%20%28Austin%29.pdf

Austin, A. E., & Sorcinelli, M. D. (2013). The future of faculty development: Where are we going? In C. W. McKee, M. Johnson, W. F. Ritchie, & W. M. Tew (Eds.), *New directions for teaching and learning: No. 133. The breadth of current faculty development: Practitioners' perspectives* (pp. 85–97). San Francisco, CA: Jossey-Bass.

Bahr, P. R. (2013). The deconstructive approach to understanding community college students' pathways and outcomes. *Community College Review, 41*(2), 137–153.

Bailey, T. R., Jaggars, S. S., & Jenkins, D. (2015). *Redesigning America's community colleges.* Boston, MA: Harvard University Press.

Baker, R. S., & Yacef, K. (2009). The state of educational data mining in 2009: A review and future visions. *Journal of Educational Data Mining, 1*(1), 3–17.

Balcer, Y., & Lippman, S. A. (1984). Technological expectations and adoption of improved technology. *Journal of Economic Theory, 34*(2), 292–318.

Baltaci-Goktalay, S., & Ocak, M. A. (2006). Faculty adoption of online technology in higher education. *Turkish Online Journal of Educational Technology, 5*(4), 37–43.

Bandura, A. (1997). *Self-efficacy: The exercise of control.* New York, NY: Freeman.

Barth, A., Datta, A., Mitchell, J. C., & Nissenbaum, H. (2006, May). Privacy and contextual integrity: Framework and applications. *2006 IEEE Symposium on Security and Privacy.* Washington, DC: IEEE Computer Society, 184–198.

Bastedo, M. N. (2009). Convergent institutional logics in public higher education: State policymaking and governing board activism. *The Review of Higher Education, 32*(2), 209–234.

Beattie, S., Woodley, C., & Souter, K. (2014). Creepy analytics and learner data rights. In B. Hegarty, J. McDonald, & S.-K. Loke (Eds.), *Rhetoric and reality: Critical perspectives on educational technology. Proceedings ASCILITE 2014.* Tugun, Queensland, Australia: ASCILITE, 421–425.

Beleche, T., Fairris, D., & Marks, M. (2012). Do course evaluations truly reflect student learning? Evidence from an objectively graded post-test. *Economics of Education Review, 31*(5), 709–719.

Ben-Naim, D., Bain, M., & Marcus, N. (2009). *A user-driven and data-driven approach for supporting teachers in reflection and adaptation of adaptive tutorials.* Presented at the Second International Conference on Educational Data Mining.

Berger, P. L., & Luckmann, T. (1966). *The social construction of reality: A treatise in the sociology of knowledge* (No. 10). London, England: Penguin Books.

Bergquist, W. H. (1992). *The four cultures of the academy.* San Francisco, CA: Jossey-Bass.

Bichsel, J. (2012). *Analytics in higher education: Benefits, barriers, progress, and recommendations (Research report).* Louisville, CO: EDUCAUSE Center for Applied Research. Retrieved from https://library.educause.edu/~/media/files/library/2012/6/ers1207.pdf?la=en

Birnbaum, R., & Edelson, P. J. (1989). How colleges work: The cybernetics of academic organization and leadership. *Journal of Continuing Higher Education, 37*(3), 27–29.

Bloom, B. S., & Krathwohl, D. R. (1956). *Taxonomy of educational objectives: The classification of educational goals, by a committee of college and university examiners. Handbook 1: Cognitive domain.* New York, NY: Longmans.

Bozdag, E. (2013). Bias in algorithmic filtering and personalization. *Ethics and Information Technology, 15*(3), 209–227.

Brown, M., Dehoney, J., & Millichap, N. (2015). *The next generation digital learning environment: A report on research.* Louisville, CO: EDUCAUSE Learning Initiative.

Brownell, S. E., & Tanner, K. D. (2012). Barriers to faculty pedagogical change: Lack of training, time, incentives, and...tensions with professional identity? *CBE-Life Sciences Education, 11,* 339–346.

Campbell, C. M., & Cabrera, A. F. (2011). How sound is NSSE?: Investigating the psychometric properties of NSSE at a public, research-extensive institution. *The Review of Higher Education, 35*(1), 77–103.

Campbell, J. P., Finnegan, C., & Collins, B. (2006). *Academic analytics: Using the CMS as an early warning system.* Paper presented at the WebCT Impact Conference 2006.

Charleer, S., Klerkx, J., Odriozola, S., Luis, J., & Duval, E. (2013, December). Improving awareness and reflection through collaborative, interactive visualizations of badges. In *ARTEL13: Proceedings of the 3rd Workshop on Awareness and Reflection in Technology-Enhanced Learning* (Vol. 1103). CEUR-WS, 69–81.

Chemers, M. M., Hu, L. T., & Garcia, B. F. (2001). Academic self-efficacy and first year college student performance and adjustment. *Journal of Educational Psychology, 93*(1), 55–64.

Coffield, F., Moseley, D., & Hall, E. (2004). *Should we be using learning styles?: What research has to say to practice.* London, England: Learning and Skills Research Centre.

Cohen, A. M., Brawer, F. B., & Kisker, C. (2013). *The American community college.* San Francisco, CA: Jossey Bass.

Coll, S., Glassey, O., & Balleys, C. (2011). Building social networks ethics beyond "privacy": a sociological perspective. *International Review of Information Ethics, 16*(12), 47–53.

Cormack, A. N. (2016). A data protection framework for learning analytics. *Journal of Learning Analytics, 3*(1), 91–106.

Crookston, B. B. (1994). A developmental view of academic advising as teaching. *NACADA Journal, 14*(2), 5–9.

Dahlstrom, E., Brooks, D. C., & Bichsel, J. (2014). *The current ecosystem of learning management systems in higher education: student, faculty, and IT perspectives (Research report).* Louisville, CO: EDUCAUSE.

Daries, J. P., Reich, J., Waldo, J., Young, E. M., Whittinghill, J., Ho, A. D., ... Chuang, I. (2014). Privacy, anonymity, and big data in the social sciences. *Communications of the ACM, 57*(9), 56–63.

D'Avanzo, C. (2013). Post–vision and change: Do we know how to change? *CBE-Life Sciences Education, 12*(3), 373–382.

Davis, F. (1989). Perceived usefulness, perceived ease of use, and user acceptance of information technology. *MIS Quarterly, 13*, 319–340.

Dawson, S. P., Macfadyen, L., & Lockyer, L. (2009). Learning or performance: Predicting drivers of student motivation. In R. Atkinson & C. McBeath (Eds.), *ASCILITE 2009: Same places, different spaces* (pp. 184–193). Tugun, Queensland, Australia: ASCILITE.

Dawson, S., McWilliam, E., & Tan, J. P. L. (2008). Teaching smarter: How mining ICT data can inform and improve learning and teaching practice. In *Hello! Where are you in the landscape of educational technology? Proceedings ASCILITE Melbourne 2008*. Tugun, Queensland, Australia: ASCILITE, 221–230. Retrieved from http://www.ascilite.org/conferences/melbourne08/procs/dawson.pdf

DeMauro, A., Greco, M., & Grimaldi, M. (2016). A formal definition of big data based on its essential features. *Library Review, 65*(3), 122–135. https://doi.org/10.1108/LR-06-2015-0061

Demmans Epp, C. D., & Bull, S. (2015). Uncertainty representation in visualizations of learning analytics for learners: Current approaches and opportunities. *IEEE Transactions on Learning Technologies, 8*(3), 242–260.

Diakopoulos, N. (2015). Algorithmic accountability: Journalistic investigation of computational power structures. *Digital Journalism, 3*(3), 398–415.

Dowd, A. C., Sawatzky, M., & Korn, R. (2011). Theoretical foundations and a research agenda to validate measures of intercultural effort. *The Review of Higher Education, 35*(1), 17–44.

Drachsler, H., & Greller, W. (2012). Confidence in learning analytics. *Proceedings of the Second International Conference on Learning Analytics & Knowledge*. New York, NY: Association for Computing Machinery, 89–98.

Drachsler, H., & Greller, W. (2016, April). Privacy and analytics: It's a DELICATE issue a checklist for trusted learning analytics. *Proceedings of the Sixth International Conference on Learning Analytics & Knowledge*. New York, NY: Association for Computing Machinery, 89–98.

Drachsler, H., Hoel, T., Scheffel, M., Kismihók, G., Berg, A., Ferguson, R., … Manderveld, J. (2015, March). Ethical and privacy issues in the application of learning analytics. *Proceedings of the Fifth International Conference on Learning Analytics and Knowledge*. New York, NY: Association for Computing Machinery, 390–391.

Dusick, D. M. (1998). What social cognitive factors influence faculty members' use of computers for teaching? A literature review. *Journal of Research on Computing in Education, 31*(2), 123–137.

Duval, E. (2011, February). Attention please!: Learning analytics for visualization and recommendation. *Proceedings of the 1st International Conference on Learning Analytics and Knowledge*. New York, NY: Association of Computing Machinery, 9–17.

Eckel, P. D., & Kezar, A. J. (2003). *Taking the reins: Institutional transformation in higher education*. Westport, CT: Greenwood Publishing Group.

Eddy, P. L. (2012). *Community college leadership: A multidimensional model for leading change*. Sterling, VA: Stylus Publishing.

Eduventures. (2013). *Predictive analytics in higher education: Data driven decision-making for the student life cycle (White paper)*. Boston, MA: Eduventures. Retrieved from http://www.eduventures.com/wp-content/uploads/2013/02/Eduventures_Predictive_Analytics_White_Paper1.pdf

Elbadrawy, A., Polyzou, A., Ren, Z., Sweeney, M., Karypis, G., & Rangwala, H. (2016). Predicting student performance using personalized analytics. *Computer, 49*(4), 61–69.

Engle, J., & Lynch, M. (2009). *Charting a necessary path: The baseline report of public higher education systems in the access to success initiative.* Washington, DC: Education Trust.

Ertmer, P. A. (2005). Teacher pedagogical beliefs: The final frontier in our quest for technology integration? *Educational Technology Research and Development, 53*(4), 25–39.

Ertmer, P. A., Ottenbreit-Leftwich, A. T., Sadik, O., Sendurur, E., & Sendurur, P. (2012). Teacher beliefs and technology integration practices: A critical relationship. *Computers & Education, 59*, 423–435.

Fairweather, J. S. (2002). The mythologies of faculty productivity: Implications for institutional policy and decision-making. *Journal of Higher Education, 73*, 26–48.

Fairweather, J. (2008). *Linking evidence and promising practices in science, technology, engineering, and mathematics (STEM) undergraduate education. A status report for the Board of Science Education, National Research Council.* Washington, DC: The National Academies.

Ferguson, R. (2012). Learning analytics: Drivers, developments and challenges. *International Journal of Technology Enhanced Learning, 4*(5–6), 304–317.

Ferguson, R., Hoel, T., Scheffel, M., & Drachsler, H. (2016). Guest editorial: Ethics and privacy in learning analytics. *Journal of Learning Analytics, 3*(1), 5–15.

Friedland, R., & Alford, R. R. (1991). Bringing society back in: Symbols, practices and institutional contradictions. In W. Powell & P. DiMaggio (Eds.), *The new institutionalism in organizational analysis* (pp. 232–263). Chicago, IL: The University of Chicago Press.

Gašević, D., Dawson, S., & Jovanović, J. (2016). Ethics and privacy as enablers of learning analytics. *Journal of Learning Analytics, 3*(1), 1–4.

Gillespie, T. (2012). Can an algorithm be wrong? *Limn, 1*(2).

Goos, M., & Salomons, A. (2016). Measuring teaching quality in higher education: Assessing selection bias in course evaluations. *Research in Higher Education, 4*(58), 341–364.

Grush, M. (2012, September 5). Community colleges leverage predictive analytics. *Campus Technology.* Retrieved from https://campustechnology.com/articles/2012/09/05/community-colleges-leverage-predictive-analytics.aspx

Hagedorn, L. S., & DuBray, D. (2010). Math and science success and nonsuccess: Journeys within the community college. *Journal of Women and Minorities in Science and Engineering, 16*(1), 31–50.

Hagen, P. L., & Jordan, P. (2008). Theoretical foundations of academic advising. In V. N. Gordon, W. R. Habley, & T. J. Grites (Eds.), *Academic advising: A comprehensive handbook* (2nd ed., pp. 17–35). San Francisco, CA: Jossey-Bass.

Hajian, S., Bonchi, F., & Castillo, C. (2016). Algorithmic bias: From discrimination discovery to fairness-aware data mining. *Proceedings of the 22nd ACM SIGKDD International Conference on Knowledge Discovery and Data Mining.* New York, NY: Association for Computing Machinery, 2125–2126.

Hall, G. E. (1979). The concerns-based approach to facilitating change. *Educational Horizons, 57*, 202–208.

Heath, J. (2014). Contemporary privacy theory contributions to learning analytics. *Journal of Learning Analytics, 1*(1), 140–149.

Hora, M. T., Bouwma-Gearhart, J., & Park, H. J. (2014). *Exploring data-driven decision-making in the field: How faculty use data and other forms of information to guide instructional decision-making* (WCER Working Paper No. 2014-3). Madison:

University of Wisconsin–Madison, Wisconsin Center for Education Research. Retrieved fromhttps://wcer.wisc.edu/docs/working-papers/Working_Paper_No_2014_03.pdf

Hora, M. T., & Holden, J. (2013). Exploring the role of instructional technology in course planning and classroom teaching: Implications for pedagogical reform. *Journal of Computing in Higher Education, 25,* 68–92.

Hughes, J. (2005). The role of teacher knowledge and learning experiences in forming technology-integrated pedagogy. *Journal of Technology and Teacher Education, 13*(2), 277.

Irvin, M., & Longmire, J. (2016). Motivating and supporting faculty in new technology-based student success initiatives: An exploration of case studies on technology acceptance. *Journal of Student Success and Retention, 3*(1), 1–25.

Jackall, R. (1988). *Moral mazes.* Hoboken, NJ: John Wiley & Sons, Ltd.

Jacob, B. A. (2005). Accountability, incentives and behavior: The impact of high-stakes testing in the Chicago Public Schools. *Journal of Public Economics, 89*(5), 761–796.

Jaffee, D. (1998). Institutionalized resistance to asynchronous learning networks. *Journal of Asynchronous Learning Networks, 2,* 21–32.

Jayaprakash, S. M., Moody, E. W., Lauría, E. J., Regan, J. R., & Baron, J. D. (2014). Early alert of academically at-risk students: An open source analytics initiative. *Journal of Learning Analytics, 1*(1), 6–47.

Kagan, D. M. (1992). Implication of research on teacher belief. *Educational Psychologist, 27*(1), 65–90.

Kay, D., Korn, N., & Oppenheim, C. (2012). Legal risk and ethical aspects of analytics in higher education. *Center for Educational Technology & Interoperability Standards, 1*(6). Retrieve from http://publications.cetis.ac.uk/2012/500

Kezar, A. (2001). *Understanding and facilitating organizational change in the 21st century. [ASHE-ERIC Higher Education Report, 28(4)].* San Francisco, CA: Jossey-Bass.

Kezar, A. (2014). *How colleges change: Understanding, leading, and enacting change.* New York, NY: Routledge.

Kezar, A., Carducci, R., & Contreras-McGavin, M. (2006). *Rethinking the "L" word in higher education: The revolution of research on leadership. [ASHE Higher Education Report, 31(6)].* San Francisco, CA: Jossey-Bass.

Kezar, A. J., & Eckel, P. D. (2002). The effect of institutional culture on change strategies in higher education: Universal principles or culturally responsive concepts? *Journal of Higher Education, 73,* 435–460.

Kezar, A. J., & Lester, J. (2009). *Organizing higher education for collaboration: A guide for campus leaders.* San Francisco, CA: Jossey-Bass.

Khalil, H., & Ebner, M. (2014, June). MOOCs completion rates and possible methods to improve retention-a literature review. In J. Viteli & M. Leikomaa (Eds.), *Proceedings of Ed-Media: World Conference on Educational Multimedia, Hypermedia and Telecommunications.* Waynesville, NC: Association for the Advancement of Computing in Education, 1305–1313.

Kim, C., Kim, M. K., Lee, C., Spector, J. M., & DeMeester, K. (2013). Teacher beliefs and technology integration. *Teaching and Teacher Education, 29,* 76–85.

Klein, C., Lester, J., Rangwala, H., & Johri, A. (2016a). *Educational technology tool adoption in higher education: User trust and evaluation.* Manuscript submitted for publication and currently under review.

Klein, C., Lester, J., Rangwala, H., & Johri, A. (2016b). *How professional beliefs, behaviors and concerns impact educational technology tool adoption*. Manuscript submitted for publication and currently under review.

Klein, C., Lester, J., Rangwala, H., & Johri, A. (2017). *Learning dashboards: How data accuracy, context and trust impact student sensemaking and learning behaviors*. Manuscript in preparation.

Klein, C., Lester, J., Rangwala, H., & Johri, A. (in press). Adoption of educational technology tools in higher education at the intersection of institutional commitment and individual trust. *Review of Higher Education*.

Kosba, E., Dimitrova, V., & Boyle, R. (2005, July). Using student and group models to support teachers in web-based distance education. In W. Nejdl, J. Kay, P. Pu, & E. Herder (Eds.), *Adaptive hypermedia and adaptive web-based systems. 5th International Conference on User Modeling*. Berlin, Germany: Springer, 124–133.

Kraemer, F., Van Overveld, K., & Peterson, M. (2011). Is there an ethics of algorithms? *Ethics and Information Technology, 13*(3), 251–260.

Krathwohl, D. R. (2002). A revision of Bloom's taxonomy: An overview. *Theory into Practice, 41*(4), 212–218.

Kuh, G. D. (2001). Assessing what really matters to student learning inside the national survey of student engagement. *Change: The Magazine of Higher Learning, 33*(3), 10–17.

Kuh, G. D. (2003). What we're learning about student engagement from NSSE: Benchmarks for effective educational practices. *Change: The Magazine of Higher Learning, 35*(2), 24–32.

Kuh, G. D. (2008). *Excerpt from high-impact educational practices: What they are, who has access to them, and why they matter*. Washington, DC: Association of American Colleges and Universities.

Kuh, G. D., Kinzie, J., Schuh, J. H., & Whitt, E. J. (2011). *Student success in college: Creating conditions that matter*. Hoboken, NJ: John Wiley & Sons.

Lake, P. F. (1999). The rise of duty and the fall of in loco parentis and other protective tort doctrines in higher education law. *Missouri Law Review, 64*, 1.

Laney, D. (2001). 3D data management: Controlling data volume, velocity and variety. *META Group Research Note, 6*, 70.

Lang, L., & Piriani, J. (2014). *The learning management system evolution*. CDS Spotlight Report. Louisville, CO: EDUCAUSE Center for Analysis and Research.

Lester, J., Brown Leonard, J., & Mathias, D. (2013). Transfer student engagement: Blurring of social and academic engagement. *Community College Review, 41*(3), 202–222.

Lester, J., Klein, C., Rangwala, H., & Johri, A. (Eds.). (in press). *Learning analytics in higher education: Current innovations, future potential, and practical applications*. New York, NY: Routledge.

Liu, S. H. (2011). Factors related to pedagogical beliefs of teachers and technology integration. *Computers & Education, 56*, 1012–1022.

Locke, L. (1995). An analysis of prospects for changing faculty roles and rewards: Can scholarship be reconsidered? *Quest, 47*, 506–524.

Lockyer, L., Heathcote, E., & Dawson, S. (2013). Informing pedagogical action: Aligning learning analytics with learning design. *American Behavioral Scientist, 57*(10), 1439–1459.

Lyon, D. (2007). *Surveillance studies: An overview*. Cambridge, UK: Polity Press.

Macfadyen, L. P., & Dawson, S. (2010). Mining LMS data to develop an "early warning system" for educators: A proof of concept. *Computers & Education, 54*(2), 588–599.

Macfadyen, L. P., & Dawson, S. (2012). Numbers are not enough. Why e-learning analytics failed to inform an institutional strategic plan. *Journal of Educational Technology & Society, 15*(3), 149–163.

Macfadyen, L. P., Dawson, S., Pardo, A., & Gašević, D. (2014). Embracing big data in complex educational systems: The learning analytics imperative and the policy challenge. *Research & Practice in Assessment, 9*, 17–28.

Mazza, R., & Dimitrova, V. (2007). CourseVis: A graphical student monitoring tool for supporting instructors in web-based distance courses. *International Journal of Human-Computer Studies, 65*, 125–139.

Meltzer, D. E., & Manivannan, K. (2002). Transforming the lecture-hall environment: The fully interactive physics lecture. *American Journal of Physics, 70*, 639–654.

National Center for Education Statistics. (2016a). Integrated postsecondary education data system (IPEDS), spring 2016, fall enrollment component; and fall 2014, institutional characteristics component. Table 326.30. *Digest of Education Statistics 2016.* Washington, DC: U.S. Department of Education. Retrieved from https://nces.ed.gov/programs/digest/d16/tables/dt16_326.30.asp

National Center for Education Statistics. (2016b). Undergraduate retention and graduation rates. *The condition of education 2016 (NCES 2016–144).* Washington, DC: U.S. Department of Education. Retrieved from https://nces.ed.gov/programs/coe/indicator_ctr.asp

National Student Clearinghouse. (2016). *Snapshot report—persistence and education.* Washington, DC: National Student Clearinghouse Research Center. Retrieved from https://nscresearchcenter.org/snapshotreport-persistenceretention22/

Nissenbaum, H. (2004). Privacy as contextual integrity. *Washington Law Review, 79*(119), 101–139.

Nodine, T., Venezia, A., & Bracco, K. R. (2011). *Changing course: A guide to increasing student completion in community colleges.* San Francisco, CA: WestEd.

Norris, D. M., & Baer, L. L. (2013). *Building organizational capacity for analytics.* Louisville, CO: EDUCAUSE Center for Applied Research. Retrieved from https://library.educause.edu/resources/2013/2/building-organizational-capacity-for-analytics

Ottenbreit-Leftwich, A. T., Glazewski, K. D., Newby, T. J., & Ertmer, P. A. (2010). Teacher value beliefs associated with using technology: Addressing professional and student needs. *Computers & Education, 55*, 1321–1335.

Pache, A. C., & Santos, F. (2010). When worlds collide: The internal dynamics of organizational responses to conflicting institutional demands. *Academy of Management Review, 35*(3), 455–476.

Pajares, M. F. (1992). Teachers' beliefs and educational research: Cleaning up a messy construct. *Review of Educational Research, 62*(3), 307–332.

Palen, L., & Dourish, P. (2003). Unpacking privacy for a networked world. *Proceedings of the SIGCHI Conference on Human Factors in Computing Systems.* New York, NY: Association for Computing Machinery, 129–136.

Pardo, A., & Siemens, G. (2014). Ethical and privacy principles for learning analytics. *British Journal of Educational Technology, 45*(3), 438–450.

Park, Y., & Jo, I. H. (2015). Development of the learning analytics dashboard to support students' learning performance. *Journal of Universal Computer Science, 21*(1), 110–133.

Peña-Ayala, A. (2014). Educational data mining: A survey and a data mining-based analysis of recent works. *Expert Systems with Applications, 41*, 1432–1462.

Petersen, R. J. (2012). Policy Dimensions of Analytics in Higher Education. *Educause Review*, *47*(4), 44.

Picciano, A. G. (2012). The evolution of big data and learning analytics in American higher education. *Journal of Asynchronous Learning Networks, 16*(3), 9–20.

Porter, S. R., & Umbach, P. D. (2006). Student survey response rates across institutions: Why do they vary? *Research in Higher Education, 47*(2), 229–247.

Prinsloo, P., & Slade, S. (2013, April). An evaluation of policy frameworks for addressing ethical considerations in learning analytics. In D. Suthers, K. Verbert, E. Duval, & X. Ochoa (Eds.), *Proceedings of the Third International Conference on Learning Analytics and Knowledge*. New York, NY: Association for Computing Machinery, 240–244.

Prinsloo, P., & Slade, S. (2015, March). Student privacy self-management: Implications for learning analytics. *Proceedings of the Fifth International Conference on Learning Analytics and Knowledge*. New York, NY: Association for Computing Machinery, 83–92.

Privateer, P. M. (1999). Academic technology and the future of higher education: Strategic paths taken and not taken. *Journal of Higher Education, 70*(1), 60–79.

Pursel, B. K., Zhang, L., Jablokow, K. W., Choi, G. W., & Velegol, D. (2016). Understanding MOOC students: Motivations and behaviours indicative of MOOC completion. *Journal of Computer Assisted Learning, 32*(3), 202–217.

Rogers, E. (1995). *Diffusion of innovations* (4th ed.). New York, NY: Free Press.

Ren, Z., Rangwala, H., & Johri, A. (2016). Predicting performance on MOOC assessments using multi-regression models. *arXiv preprint arXiv:1605.02269*.

Rubel, A., & Jones, K. M. (2016). Student privacy in learning analytics: An information ethics perspective. *The Information Society, 32*(2), 143–159.

Santos, J. L., Verbert, K., Govaerts, S., & Duval, E. (2013, April). Addressing learner issues with StepUp!: An evaluation. In D. Suthers, K. Verbert, E. Duval, & X. Ochoa (Eds.), *Proceedings of the Third International Conference on Learning Analytics and Knowledge*. New York, NY: Association of Computing Machinery, 14–22.

Sclater, N. (2016). Developing a code of practice for learning analytics. *Journal of Learning Analytics, 3*(1), 16–42.

Sclater, N., & Bailey, P. (2015). *Code of practice for learning analytics*. London, UK: JISC.

Sclater, N., Peasgood, A., & Mullan, J. (2016). *Case study A: Traffic lights and interventions: Signals at Purdue University*. Bristol, UK: JISC. Retrieved from https://analytics.jiscinvolve.org/wp/files/2016/04/CASE-STUDY-A-Purdue-University.pdf

Selingo, J. J. (2013). *College (un) bound: The future of higher education and what it means for students*. Boston, MA: Houghton Mifflin Harcourt.

Siemens, G. (2012, April). Learning analytics: envisioning a research discipline and a domain of practice. In S. B. Shum, D. Gašević, & R. Ferguson (Eds.), *Proceedings of the Second International Conference on Learning Analytics and Knowledge*. New York, NY: Association for Computing Machinery, 4–8.

Siemens, G., & Gašević, D. (2012). Guest editorial-learning and knowledge analytics. *Educational Technology & Society, 15*(3), 1–2.

Siemens, G., & Long, P. (2011). Penetrating the fog: Analytics in learning and education. *EDUCAUSE Review, 46*(5), 30.

Slade, S., & Prinsloo, P. (2013). Learning analytics ethical issues and dilemmas. *American Behavioral Scientist, 57*(10), 1510–1529.

Slade, S., & Prinsloo, P. (2015). Student perspectives on the use of their data: Between intrusion, surveillance and care. *European Journal of Open, Distance and E-learning, 18*(1), 291–300.

Slaughter, S., & Rhoades, G. (2004). *Academic capitalism and the new economy: Markets, state, and higher education.* Baltimore, MD: Johns Hopkins University Press.

Steiner, C. M., Kickmeier-Rust, M. D., & Albert, D. (2016). LEA in private: A privacy and data protection framework for a learning analytics toolbox. *Journal of Learning Analytics, 3*(1), 66–90.

Stokes, D. E. (2011). *Pasteur's quadrant: Basic science and technological innovation.* Washington, DC: Brookings Institution Press.

Straub, E. T. (2009). Understanding technology adoption: Theory and future directions for informal learning. *Review of Educational Research, 79*(2), 625–649.

Sunal, D. W., Hodges, J., Sunal, C. S., Whitaker, K. W., Freeman, L. M., Edwards, L., ... Odell, M. (2001). Teaching science in higher education: Faculty professional development and barriers to change. *School Science and Mathematics, 101*, 246–257.

Sweeney, M., Lester, J., & Rangwala, H. (2015, October). Next-term student grade prediction. *2015 IEEE International Conference on Big Data (Big Data).* Washington, DC: IEEE Computer Society, 970–975.

Swenson, J. (2014, March). Establishing an ethical literacy for learning analytics. *Proceedings of the Fourth International Conference on Learning Analytics and Knowledge.* New York, NY: Association for Computing Machinery, 246–250.

Tagg, J. (2012). Why does the faculty resist change? *Change: The Magazine of Higher Learning, 44*(1), 6–15.

Tene, O., & Polonetsky, J. (2013). Big data for all: Privacy and user control in the age of analytics. *Northwestern Journal of Technology & Intellectual Property, 11*(5).

Thornton, P. H., & Ocasio, W. (1999). Institutional logics and the historical contingency of power in organizations: Executive succession in the higher education publishing industry, 1958–1990. *American Journal of Sociology, 105*(3), 801–843.

Thornton, P. H., & Ocasio, W. (2008). Institutional logics. In R. Greenwood, C. Oliver, R. Suddaby, & K. Sahlin-Andersson (Eds.), *The SAGE handbook of organizational institutionalism* (pp. 99–129). Los Angeles, CA: SAGE.

Tinto, V. (1987). *Leaving college: Rethinking the causes and cures of student attrition.* Chicago, IL: University of Chicago Press.

Treischl, E., & Wolbring, T. (2017). The causal effect of survey mode on students' evaluations of teaching: Empirical evidence from three field experiments. *Research in Higher Education,* 1–18.

Venkatesh, V., & Bala, H. (2008). Technology acceptance model 3 and a research agenda on interventions. *Decision Sciences, 39*, 273–315.

Venkatesh, V., Morris, M. G., Davis, G. B., & Davis, F. D. (2003). User acceptance of information technology: Toward a unified view. *MIS Quarterly, 27*(3), 425–478.

Verbert, K., Duval, E., Klerkx, J., Govaerts, S., & Santos, J. L. (2013). Learning analytics dashboard applications. *American Behavioral Scientist, 57*(10), 1500–1509.

Verbert, K., Govaerts, S., Duval, E., Santos, J. L., Assche, F., Parra, G., & Klerkx, J. (2014). Learning dashboards: An overview and future research opportunities. *Personal and Ubiquitous Computing, 18*(6), 1499–1514.

Wang, R., Chen, F., Chen, Z., Li, T., Harari, G., Tignor, S., … Campbell, A. T. (2014, September). StudentLife: Assessing mental health, academic performance and behavioral trends of college students using smartphones. *Proceedings of the 2014 ACM International Joint Conference on Pervasive and Ubiquitous Computing*. New York, NY: Association of Computing Machinery, 3–14.

Westin, A. F. (1968). Privacy and freedom. *Washington and Lee Law Review, 25*(1), 166.

Wieman, C. (2015). A better way to evaluate undergraduate teaching. *Change: The Magazine of Higher Learning, 47*(1), 6–15.

Wieman, C. (2017). *Improving how universities teach science: Lessons from the Science Education Initiative*. Cambridge, MA: Harvard University Press.

Willingham, D. T., Hughes, E. M., & Dobolyi, D. G. (2015). The scientific status of learning styles theories. *Teaching of Psychology, 42*(3), 266–271.

Willis, J. E. (2014, August). Learning analytics and ethics: A framework beyond utilitarianism. *EDUCAUSE Review*. Retrieved from http://www.educause.edu/ero/article/learning-analytics-and-ethics-framework-beyond-utilitarianism

Willis, J. E. III, Campbell, J., & Pistilli, M.D. (2013). Ethics, big data, and analytics: A model for application. *EDUCAUSE Review*. Retrieved from http://er.educause.edu/articles/2013/5/ethics-big-data-and-analytics-a-model-for-application

Willis, J. E. III, & Pistilli, M. D. (2014, April). Ethical discourse: Guiding the future of learning analytics. *EDUCAUSE Review*. Retrieved from http://er.educause.edu/articles/2014/4/ethical-discourse-guiding-the-future-of-learning-analytics

Wolbring, T., & Treischl, E. (2016). Selection bias in students' evaluation of teaching. *Research in Higher Education, 57*(1), 51–71.

Ylijoki, O., & Porras, J. (2016). Perspectives to definition of big data: A mapping study and discussion. *Journal of Innovation Management, 4*(1), 69–91.

Zellweger-Moser, F. (2007a). Faculty adoption of educational technology. *EDUCAUSE Quarterly, 30*(1), 66–69.

Zellweger-Moser, F. (2007b). *The strategic management of e-learning support*. New York, NY: Waxmann Münster.

Zwitter, A. (2014, July–December). Big data ethics. *Big Data & Society*, (16). https://doi.org/10.1177/2053951714559253

Name Index

A

Adams, M. J., 117
Adelman, C., 24
Albert, D., 74
Alexander, F. K., 100
Alford, R. R., 46
Ali, L., 10, 26, 28, 53
Almatrafi, O., 24
Amey, M. J., 32, 38, 41, 60, 63, 101
Andrejevic, M., 34
Appleby, D. C., 33, 40, 60
Arnold, K. E., 12, 13, 23, 28, 29, 31, 33, 38, 39, 44, 48, 49, 66, 67, 100, 105
Arroway, P., 19, 20, 27
Assche, F., 28, 34, 66, 67
Astin, A. W., 22
Austin, A. E., 10, 12, 13, 31, 32, 33, 38, 40, 41, 42, 43, 44, 46, 49, 53, 60, 61, 62, 63, 102

B

Baer, L. L., 10, 12, 13, 26, 29, 31, 33, 38, 39, 44, 48, 49, 53, 59, 60, 66, 100
Bahr, P. R., 24
Bailey, P., 95
Bailey, T. R., 23
Bain, M., 33
Baker, R. S., 33, 66
Bala, H., 62
Balcer, Y., 50
Balleys, C., 34

Baltaci-Goktalay, S., 44
Bandura, A., 65
Baron, J. D., 28
Barth, A., 78
Bastedo, M. N., 44, 46, 100
Beattie, S., 88, 94, 95
Beleche, T., 117
Ben-Naim, D., 33, 66
Berg, A., 75, 109
Berger, P. L., 47
Bergquist, W. H., 32
Bichsel, J., 12, 13, 31, 33, 38, 44, 53, 59, 60, 66
Birnbaum, R., 32
Bloom, B. S., 116
Bonchi, F., 86
Bouwma-Gearhart, J., 28, 54, 102
Boyle, R., 28
Bozdag, E., 86
Bracco, K. R., 24
Brawer, F. B., 22
Brooks, D. C., 13
Brownell, S. E., 31, 32, 33, 60, 63
Brown Leonard, J., 115
Brown, M., 107
Bull, S., 69, 70

C

Cabrera, A. F., 115
Campbell, A. T., 116
Campbell, C. M., 115

Campbell, J., 83
Campbell, J. P., 24
Carducci, R., 101
Castillo, C., 86
Charleer, S., 69
Chemers, M. M., 65
Chen, F., 116
Chen, Z., 116
Choi, G.W., 25
Chuang, I., 91
Coffield, F., 116
Cohen, A. M., 22
Collins, B., 24
Coll, S., 34
Contreras-McGavin, M., 101
Cormack, A. N., 95
Crookston, B. B., 33, 40, 60

D

Dahlstrom, E., 13, 33, 38, 53, 54, 59, 60, 66, 101
Daries, J. P., 91
Datta, A., 78
D'Avanzo, C., 32, 33, 60, 61
Davis, F., 32, 50
Davis, F. D., 32, 50
Davis, G. B., 32, 50
Dawson, S., 10, 12, 13, 25, 26, 28, 31, 33, 38, 44, 53, 54, 59, 66, 75, 103
Dawson, S. P., 20
Dehoney, J., 107
DeMauro, A., 9, 18
DeMeester, K., 33
Demmans Epp, C. D., 69, 70
Diakopoulos, N., 86, 87
Dimitrova, V., 28, 33, 66
Dobolyi, D. G., 116
Dourish, P., 78
Dowd, A. C., 115
Drachsler, H., 75, 109
DuBray, D., 24
Dusick, D.M., 43
Duval, E., 28, 34, 66, 67

E

Ebner, M., 75

Eckel, P. D., 32, 100
Eddy, P. L., 101
Edelson, P. J., 32
Edwards, L., 32, 33, 60, 61
Elbadrawy, A., 24
Engle, J., 100
Ertmer, P. A., 32, 33, 62
Ewell, P., 24

F

Fairris, D., 117
Fairweather, J., 31, 33, 39, 42, 43, 60, 61, 63
Fairweather, J. S., 31, 60, 63
Ferguson, R., 75, 109
Finnegan, C., 24
Freeman, L. M., 32, 33, 60, 61
Friedland, R., 46

G

Garcia, B. F., 65
Gaston, P., 24
Geary Schneider, C., 24
Gillespie, T., 87
Glassey, O., 34
Glazewski, K. D., 33
Goos, M., 117
Govaerts, S., 28, 34, 66, 67
Greco, M., 9, 18
Greller, W., 77, 78, 80, 82, 84, 85, 88, 90, 94, 95
Grimaldi, M., 9, 18
Grush, M., 29

H

Hagedorn, L. S., 24
Hagen, P. L., 33, 40, 60
Hajian, S., 86
Hall, E., 116
Hall, G. E., 51
Harari, G., 116
Hatala, M., 10
Heathcote, E., 28, 54
Heath, J., 28, 54
Ho, A. D., 91
Hodges, J., 32, 33, 60, 61

Hoel, T., 75, 109
Holden, J., 32, 33, 39, 60, 61, 62
Hora, M. T., 28, 32, 33, 39, 54, 60, 61, 62, 102
Hughes, E. M., 116
Hughes, J., 33
Hu, L. T., 65

I

Irvin, M., 66

J

Jablokow, K.W., 25
Jackall, R., 46
Jacob, B. A., 25
Jaffee, D., 64
Jaggars, S. S., 23
Jayaprakash, S. M., 28, 34, 66, 68
Jenkins, D., 23
Johri, A., 13, 15, 24, 25, 34, 38, 45, 117
Jo, I. H., 28, 39, 66, 68, 69, 70
Jones, K. M., 29, 75, 87, 88, 91, 109
Jordan, P., 33, 40, 60

K

Kagan, D.M., 33, 61, 62
Karypis, G., 24
Kay, D., 80, 89, 90
Kezar, A., 32, 44, 45, 100, 101
Kezar, A. J., 12, 32, 38, 41, 44, 92, 101
Khalil, H., 75
Kickmeier-Rust, M. D., 74
Kim, C., 33
Kim, M. K., 33
Kinzie, J., 115
Kisker, C., 22
Kismihók, G., 75, 109
Klein, C., 12, 15, 34, 38, 39, 45, 49, 53, 54, 63, 64, 69, 86, 91, 94, 103, 105, 117
Klerkx, J., 28, 34, 66, 67
Korn, N., 80
Korn, R., 115
Kosba, E., 28
Kraemer, F., 86, 87
Krathwohl, D. R., 116

Kuh, G. D., 22, 115

L

Lake, P. F., 80
Laney, D., 9, 18
Lang, L., 24
Lauría, E. J., 28
Lee, C., 33
Lester, J., 12, 13, 15, 24, 32, 34, 38, 41, 44, 45, 92, 100, 115, 116, 117
Lippman, S. A., 50
Li, T., 116
Liu, S. H., 32, 33, 61, 62
Locke, L., 42, 60, 63
Lockyer, L., 20, 28, 53, 54
Longmire, J., 66
Long, P., 29
Lonn, S., 12, 29, 38
Luckmann, T., 47
Luis, J., 69
Lynch, M., 100
Lyon, D., 34

M

Macfadyen, L., 20
Macfadyen, L. P., 10, 12, 13, 25, 26, 31, 33, 38, 44, 59, 66
Manderveld, J., 75, 109
Manivannan, K., 62
Marcus, N., 33
Marks, M., 117
Mathias, D., 115
Mazza, R., 33, 66
McWilliam, E., 53
Meltzer, D. E., 62
Millichap, N., 107
Mitchell, J. C., 78
Moody, E. W., 28
Morgan, G., 19
Morris, M. G., 32
Moseley, D., 116
Mullan, J., 23

N

Newby, T. J., 33
Nissenbaum, H., 77, 78

Nodine, T., 24
Norris, D. M., 10, 12, 13, 26, 29, 31, 33, 38, 39, 44, 48, 49, 53, 59, 60, 66, 100

O
Ocak, M. A., 44
Ocasio, W., 46, 47
Odell, M., 32, 33, 60, 61
Odriozola, S., 69
O'Keefe, M., 19
Oppenheim, C., 80
Ottenbreit-Leftwich, A. T., 33, 61, 62

P
Pache, A. C., 46, 47
Pajares, M. F., 33
Palen, L., 78
Pardo, A., 26, 34, 74, 76, 78, 81, 83, 87, 90, 95, 109
Park, H. J., 28
Park, Y., 28, 39, 66, 68, 69, 70
Parra, G., 28, 34, 66, 67
Peasgood, A., 23
Peña-Ayala, A., 33, 66
Petersen, R. J., 34
Peterson, M., 86, 87
Picciano, A. G., 9, 18, 23
Piriani, J., 24
Pistilli, M. D., 12, 13, 23, 28, 29, 33, 38, 39, 66, 67, 75, 83, 97, 105, 109
Polonetsky, J., 87
Polyzou, A., 24
Porras, J., 9, 18
Porter, S. R., 115
Prinsloo, P., 26, 30, 34, 74, 75, 76, 79, 82, 83, 84, 85, 88, 91, 92, 93, 95, 96, 109
Privateer, P. M., 50
Pursel, B. K., 25

R
Rangwala, H., 13, 15, 24, 25, 34, 38, 45, 117
Regan, J. R., 28
Reich, J., 91
Ren, Z., 24, 25
Rhoades, G., 99

Rogers, E., 32, 50
Rubel, A., 29, 75, 87, 88, 91, 109

S
Sadik, O., 33
Salomons, A., 117
Santos, F., 46, 47
Santos, J. L., 28, 34, 66, 67
Sawatzky, M., 115
Scheffel, M., 75, 109
Schuh, J. H., 115
Sclater, N., 23, 75, 76, 95, 109
Selingo, J. J., 27
Sendurur, E., 33
Sendurur, P., 33
Siemens, G., 10, 19, 29, 34, 74, 76, 78, 81, 83, 87, 88, 90, 95, 109
Slade, S., 26, 30, 34, 74, 75, 76, 79, 82, 83, 84, 85, 88, 91, 92, 93, 95, 96, 109
Slaughter, S., 99
Sorcinelli, M. D., 10, 32, 41, 44
Souter, K., 88
Spector, J. M., 33
Steiner, C. M., 74, 75, 76, 84, 85, 87, 88, 89, 90, 91, 95, 96, 109
Stokes, D. E., 113
Straub, E. T., 32, 50
Sunal, C. S., 32, 33, 60, 61
Sunal, D. W., 32, 33, 60, 61
Sweeney, M., 24
Swenson, J., 75, 109

T
Tagg, J., 31, 60, 61, 63
Tan, J. P. L., 53
Tanner, K. D., 31, 32, 33, 60, 63
Tene, O., 87
Thornton, P. H., 46, 47
Tignor, S., 116
Tinto, V., 22
Treischl, E., 117

U
Umbach, P. D., 115, 117

V

Van Overveld, K., 86, 87
Velegol, D., 25
Venezia, A., 24
Venkatesh, V., 32, 50, 62
Verbert, K., 28, 34, 66, 67

W

Waldo, J., 91
Wang, R., 116
Westin, A. F., 77
Whitaker, K. W., 32, 33, 60, 61
Whitt, E. J., 115
Whittinghill, J., 91
Wieman, C., 117
Willingham, D. T., 116

Willis, J. E., 75, 79, 80, 109
Willis, J. E. III, 75, 83, 97, 109
Wolbring, T., 117
Woodley, C., 88

Y

Yacef, K., 33, 66
Yanosky, R., 19
Ylijoki, O., 9, 18
Young, E. M., 91

Z

Zellweger-Moser, F., 32, 51, 52, 63
Zhang, L., 25
Zwitter, A., 9, 18

Subject Index

A

Algorithmic bias, 86–87
American Graduation Initiative, 24
Association for Computing Machinery (ACM), 120
Association of American Colleges and Universities (AAC&U), 25

B

Belmont Report, 90
Blackboard Learn, 66

C

Centre for Educational Technology, Interoperability and Standards (CETIS), 120
Civitas, 66
Concerns-Based Adoption Model (CBAM), 51
Course Signals (CS), 67

D

Degree Qualification Profile, 24

E

Educational data mining (EDM), 122
EDUCAUSE, 19
Ethics and privacy, 72–76; challenges in practice, 93–94; data considerations, 86–89; definition and conception, 76–81; emerging codes of practice, 94–96; future prospectives, 96–97; individual contexts, 83–86; institutional contexts, 81–83; institutional, individual, and data considerations, 81; laws and regulations, 89–92; laws, policies, and codes of practice, 89; policies and recommendations, 92–93
European Commission (EC), 90
European Distance and E-Learning Network (EDEN), 121

F

Faculty Educational Technology Adoption Cycle (FETAC), 32, 51
Fair Information Practice Principles (FIPP), 91
Family Educational Rights and Privacy Act (FERPA), 30, 91

G

GI Bill, 80
GLASS, 66

H

Helsinki Declaration, 90
Higher education: ethics and privacy, 34; examining learning analytics in, 30–31; faculty and advisor beliefs and behaviors, 32–33; future prospectives, 54–55; individual factors, 34; institutional levels, 41–42; institutional

logics, 46–47; learning analytics research in, 27–30; organizational model, for individual decision making, 40–41; organizational readiness and capacity, 47–49; organizational theory, 31–32; student use and action, 33–34; technology adoption and alignment, 49; technology adoption models, 49–52; technology alignment and adoption, 32
Higher education, current trends in, 21–27

I
Innovation Diffusion Theory, 50

L
LAPA, 66
Learning analytics (LA), 10, 19; college student interpretation, 105–108; data access, provenance, and fidelity, 111–112; data concerns and recommendations, 111; ethical codes, 117–119; ethics and privacy, 108–110; faculty and advisor input, trust, and engagement, 102–105; future prospectives, 114; modeling student engagement, 115–116; organizational logic, leadership, and value, 99–101; Pasteur's Quadrant, 113–114; privacy, accountability, transparency, security, and trust, 114; quasiexperimental designs of intervention impacts, 115; scenario-based design of systems, 112; stakeholders, 113; visualizing student learning preferences, 116–117; work practice integration of systems, 112–113
Learning Analytics Community Exchange (LACE), 122
Learning analytics data and tools, 56–59; faculty and advisor decision making, 59–60; future prospectives, 64–65, 71; learning analytics dashboards, 65–70; professional behaviors, 62–64; professional beliefs, 61–62; professional identity, 60–61; student decision making, 65
Learning Analytics Initiative (LAI), 120

Learning Analytics & Knowledge (LAK), 75, 121, 122
Learning Analytics Readiness Instrument (LARI), 29
Learning Analytics Summer Institute (LASI), 122
Learning management systems (LMS), 9
Liberal Education and America's Promise (LEAP), 25

M
Massive open online course (MOOC), 25
Moodle, 66

N
National Center for Education Statistics (NCES), 22
National Student Clearinghouse, 22
National Survey of Student Engagement (NSSE), 115–116
No Child Left Behind, 25
Nuremberg Code, 90

O
Office of Educational Technology (OET), 122
Open Academics Analytics Initiative (OAAI), 66
Organisation for Economic Cooperation and Development (OECD), 90
Organizational Capacity for Analytics Model, 29
Otanational Science Foundation (NSF), 38

P
P–20 education-based model, 32
Potter Box, 83
Professor Smith tool, 19
Purdue Course Signals Project, 23

R
RioPACE, 66

S
Santos, 67

Science, technology, engineering, and
    mathematics (STEM), 61
SNAPP, 66
Society of Learning Analytics Research
    (SOLAR), 121, 122
Student Activity Meter (SAM), 66
Supporting Higher Education in Learning
    Analytics (SHEILA), 122

T
Technology Acceptance Model (TAM), 32,
    50

U
Universal Technology Adoption and Use
    Theory (UTAUT), 32, 50

V
Verbert, 67
Voluntary Framework for Accountability,
    25

About the Authors

Jaime Lester is an associate professor in the Higher Education Program at George Mason University. Dr. Lester holds a PhD from the University of Southern California's Rossier School of Education. The overarching goal of her research program is to examine organizational change and leadership in higher education, through examination of nonpositional leadership and tactics to promote local and institutional change and the role of individual identity in creating equitable workplaces in colleges and universities.

Carrie Klein is a PhD research and teaching assistant in the Higher Education Program at George Mason University. Her research interests include better understanding the impact of big data in higher education, specifically in the areas of interventions and individual agency; the influence of external actors on colleges and universities; and the intersections of organizational structure, power, and privilege within higher education.

Huzefa Rangwala is an associate professor in the Department of Computer Science at George Mason University. His research interests include data mining and applications in learning sciences and biomedical informatics. Dr. Rangwala received a PhD in computer science from the University of Minnesota Twin Cities.

Aditya Johri is an associate professor in the Information Sciences and Technology Department at George Mason University. Dr. Johri studies the use of information and communication technologies (ICT) for learning and knowledge sharing, with a focus on cognition in informal environments. Dr. Johri earned his PhD in Learning Sciences and Technology Design at Stanford University.

About the ASHE Higher Education Report Series

Since 1983, the ASHE (formerly ASHE-ERIC) Higher Education Report Series has been providing researchers, scholars, and practitioners with timely and substantive information on the critical issues facing higher education. Each monograph presents a definitive analysis of a higher education problem or issue, based on a thorough synthesis of significant literature and institutional experiences. Topics range from planning to diversity and multiculturalism, to performance indicators, to curricular innovations. The mission of the Series is to link the best of higher education research and practice to inform decision making and policy. The reports connect conventional wisdom with research and are designed to help busy individuals keep up with the higher education literature. Authors are scholars and practitioners in the academic community. Each report includes an executive summary, review of the pertinent literature, descriptions of effective educational practices, and a summary of key issues to keep in mind to improve educational policies and practice.

This series is one of the most peer reviewed in higher education. A National Advisory Board made up of ASHE members reviews proposals. A National Review Board of ASHE scholars and practitioners reviews completed manuscripts. Six monographs are published each year, and they are approximately 144 pages in length. The reports are widely disseminated through Jossey-Bass and John Wiley & Sons, and they are available online to subscribing institutions through Wiley Online Library (http://wileyonlinelibrary.com).

Call for Proposals

The ASHE Higher Education Report Series is actively looking for proposals. We encourage you to contact one of the editors, Dr. Kelly Ward (kaward@wsu.edu) or Dr. Lisa Wolf-Wendel (lwolf@ku.edu), with your ideas.

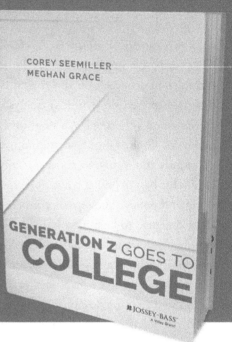

ASHE HIGHER EDUCATION REPORT

ORDER FORM SUBSCRIPTION AND SINGLE ISSUES

DISCOUNTED BACK ISSUES:

Use this form to receive 20% off all back issues of *ASHE Higher Education Report*.
All single issues priced at **$23.20** (normally $29.00)

TITLE   ISSUE NO.   ISBN

_____   _____   _____

_____   _____   _____

_____   _____   _____

Call 1-800-835-6770 or see mailing instructions below. When calling, mention the promotional code JBNND to receive your discount. For a complete list of issues, please visit www.wiley.com/WileyCDA/WileyTitle/productCd-AEHE.html

SUBSCRIPTIONS: (1 YEAR, 6 ISSUES)

☐ New Order   ☐ Renewal

U.S.	☐ Individual: $174	☐ Institutional: $347
CANADA/MEXICO	☐ Individual: $174	☐ Institutional: $437
ALL OTHERS	☐ Individual: $210	☐ Institutional: $491

Call 1-800-835-6770 or see mailing and pricing instructions below.
Online subscriptions are available at www.onlinelibrary.wiley.com

ORDER TOTALS:

Issue / Subscription Amount: $ _____

Shipping Amount: $ _____
(for single issues only – subscription prices include shipping)

Total Amount: $ _____

SHIPPING CHARGES:

First Item $6.00
Each Add'l Item $2.00

(No sales tax for U.S. subscriptions. Canadian residents, add GST for subscription orders. Individual rate subscriptions must be paid by personal check or credit card. Individual rate subscriptions may not be resold as library copies.)

BILLING & SHIPPING INFORMATION:

☐ **PAYMENT ENCLOSED:** *(U.S. check or money order only. All payments must be in U.S. dollars.)*

☐ **CREDIT CARD:**   ☐ VISA   ☐ MC   ☐ AMEX

Card number _____Exp. Date_____

Card Holder Name_____Card Issue # _____

Signature _____Day Phone_____

☐ **BILL ME:** *(U.S. institutional orders only. Purchase order required.)*

Purchase order # _____
                        Federal Tax ID 13559302 • GST 89102-8052

Name_____

Address_____

Phone_____ E-mail_____

Copy or detach page and send to: **John Wiley & Sons, Inc. / Jossey Bass**
                                    PO Box 55381
                                    Boston, MA 02205-9850

PROMO JBNND